Stand Out Basic
Grammar Challenge

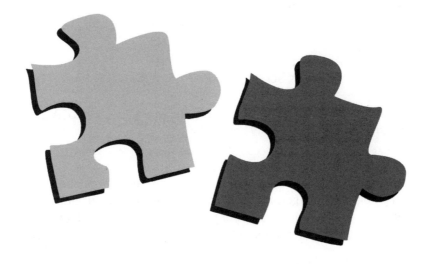

THOMSON
HEINLE

Australia • Canada • Mexico • Singapore • Spain • United Kingdom • United States

Stand Out Basic
Grammar Challenge

Publisher, Adult and Academic ESL: *James W. Brown*
Senior Acquisitions Editor: *Sherrise Roehr*
Director of Product Development: *Anita Raducanu*
Developmental Editor: *Yeni Kim*
Editorial Assistant: *Katherine Reilly*
Marketing Manager: *Donna Lee Kennedy*
Director, Global ESL Training & Development: *Evelyn Nelson*
Senior Production Editor: *Maryellen Killeen*
Senior Manufacturing Coordinator: *Mary Beth Hunnebury*
Photo Researcher: *Sheri Blaney*
Contributing Writer: *Ingrid Wisniewska*
Project Manager: *Tünde A. Dewey*
Compositor: *Pre-Press Company, Inc.*
Printer: *The West Group*
Cover Designer: *Rotunda Design/Lori Stuart*
Illustrators: *Ray Medici*
James Edwards, represented by Sheryl Beranbaum
Leo Cultura of Racketshop Design Studio, Phillippines
Scott MacNeill

Copyright © 2005 Heinle, a division of Thomson Learning, Inc.
Thomson Learning™ is a trademark used herein under license.

Printed in the United States of America.
3 4 5 6 7 8 9 10   08 07 06 05

For more information, contact Heinle, 25 Thomson Place, Boston, MA 02210 USA, or you can visit our Internet site at http://www.heinle.com

All rights reserved. No part of this work covered by the copyright hereon may be reproduced or used in any form or by any means—graphic, electronic, or mechanical, including photocopying, recording, taping, Web distribution or information storage and retrieval systems—without the written permission of the publisher.

> For permission to use material from this text or product, contact us:
> Tel   1-800-730-2214
> Fax   1-800-730-2215
> Web www.thomsonrights.com

ISBN: 1-41300-163-7
ISE ISBN 1-41300-1536-0   International Student Edition not for sale in the United States

CONTENTS

UNIT 1: Personal Information 1

CHALLENGE 1	Subject pronouns	1
CHALLENGE 2	The verb *be*	3
CHALLENGE 3	Contractions with the verb *be*	5
CHALLENGE 4	Possessive adjectives	7
CHALLENGE 5	Review	9

UNIT 2: Our Class 10

CHALLENGE 1	Where are you from?	10
CHALLENGE 2	Tell time	12
CHALLENGE 3	Prepositions	14
CHALLENGE 4	Possessive forms	16
CHALLENGE 5	Review	18

UNIT 3: Food 19

CHALLENGE 1	Negative form of the verb *be*	19
CHALLENGE 2	*A / an* and singular / plural nouns	21
CHALLENGE 3	Count and non-count nouns	23
CHALLENGE 4	Simple present of *like* and *want*	25
CHALLENGE 5	Review	27

UNIT 4: Clothing 28

CHALLENGE 1	*There is / There are*	28
CHALLENGE 2	Counting money	30
CHALLENGE 3	Questions with *How much . . . ?*	32
CHALLENGE 4	*What size / color?* and *How many . . . ?*	34
CHALLENGE 5	Review	36

UNIT 5: Our Community 37

CHALLENGE 1	Questions with *Where* . . . ?	37
CHALLENGE 2	Questions and answers with . . . "*or*" . . .	39
CHALLENGE 3	*Yes/No* questions and answers with *do*	41
CHALLENGE 4	*Where* questions and *yes/no* questions with *be*	43
CHALLENGE 5	Review	45

UNIT 6: Healthy Living 46

CHALLENGE 1	Simple present of regular and irregular verbs	46
CHALLENGE 2	Present continuous	48
CHALLENGE 3	Negative simple present of regular verbs	50
CHALLENGE 4	Questions with *How often* . . . ?	52
CHALLENGE 5	Review	54

UNIT 7: Work 55

CHALLENGE 1	*Wh-* questions with *do*	55
CHALLENGE 2	*Yes/No* questions and answers with *do*	57
CHALLENGE 3	Modal Verb: *can* and *can't*	59
CHALLENGE 4	Affirmative and negative commands	61
CHALLENGE 5	Review	63

UNIT 8: Lifelong Learning 64

CHALLENGE 1	Review: Containers / measurements with count and non-count nouns	64
CHALLENGE 2	Review: *Wh-* questions with *be* and *do*	66
CHALLENGE 3	Review: Simple present and present continuous	68
CHALLENGE 4	Review: Negative forms of *be* and *do*	70
CHALLENGE 5	Review	72

APPENDIX

GLOSSARY OF GRAMMAR TERMS	A-1
GRAMMAR REFERENCE	A-3

UNIT 1 Personal Information

CHALLENGE 1 ▶ Subject pronouns

A Write the words from the box under the pictures.

| I | you | he | she | it | we | they |

EXAMPLE: 1. __we__

2. _____

3. _____

4. _____

5. _____

6. _____

7. _____

8. _____

UNIT 1

B Circle the correct word.

EXAMPLE: 1. _____ 2. _____ is a student. 3. _____ are Josef and Anna.

(He) / She / It   He / She / It   We / You / They

4. _____ am Amal. 5. _____ are Elsa and Chinh. 6. _____ is a book.

I / You / We   I / You / We   He / She / It

7. I am Chinh and _____ is Elsa. 8. _____ are pencils. 9. _____ are a student.

He / She / They   We / You / They   I / You / We

C Complete the sentences. Use pronouns.

EXAMPLE: Amal is a student. **He** is from Egypt.

1. Elsa is a student. _____ is from Russia.
2. Amal and I are students. _____ are in the same class.
3. Mr. Jackson is a teacher. _____ is from Florida.
4. Mrs. Samuel and Mr. Jackson are from Florida. _____ are teachers.

Subject pronouns

UNIT 1 Personal Information

CHALLENGE 2 ▶ The verb *be*

be verb + noun			
Pronoun	*be* verb	Noun	Example sentence
I	am	a student	I am a student.
He / She / It	is	a teacher a friend a book	He is a teacher. She is a friend. It is a book.
We / You / They	are	friends students teachers	We are friends. You are students. They are teachers.

A Write the words from the box under the pictures. | am   is   are |

1. We ___*are*___ students.   2. It _____ a car.   3. I _____ Amal.

4. Chinh _____ a student.   5. Amal, Chinh, and Matsu _____ friends.   6. You _____ a student.

B Complete the sentences.

EXAMPLE: Mrs. Samuel ___*is*___ a teacher.

1. I _____ a student.
2. Mr. Jackson _____ a teacher.
3. Chinh and Elsa _____ students.
4. Matsu and Amal _____ students.
5. It _____ a pencil.
6. You and I _____ friends.

be verb + adjective

Pronoun	be	Adjective	Example sentence
I	am	single	I am single.
He/She	is	married divorced	He is divorced. She is married.
We/You/They	are	single married divorced	We are married. You are divorced. They are single.

C Write the words from the box under the pictures.

| am | is | are |

1. He _____ single.   2. They _____ divorced.   3. They _____ married.

D Complete the sentences with the correct *be* verb.

EXAMPLE: Amal __*is*__ single.

1. Matsu _____ married.
2. Yolanda _____ single.
3. Ron and Erika _____ divorced.
4. We _____ married.
5. Elsa _____ single.
6. You _____ married.
7. Erika and I _____ single.
8. My friend _____ divorced.
9. I _____ married.
10. They _____ divorced.

UNIT 1

UNIT 1 Personal Information

CHALLENGE 3 ▶ Contractions with the verb *be*

Subject pronoun and *be* verb	Contraction (short form)	Example sentence
I am	I'm	I'm a student.
You are	You're	You're a teacher.
She is	She's	She's a friend.
He is	He's	He's married.
It is	It's	It's Thursday.
We are	We're	We're single.
They are	They're	They're divorced.

 A Complete the sentences. Use subject pronouns and contractions of the verb *be*.

EXAMPLE: (he) ____**He's**____ a student.

1. (I) _____ Amal.   2. (she) _____ a student.   3. (we) _____ students.

4. (they) _____ friends.   5. (you) _____ a student.   6. (it) _____ a car.

UNIT 1 5

B Bubble in the correct answer.

EXAMPLE: Matsu is a student. _____ a friend. ○ We're ● He's ○ They're

1. Today is Tuesday. _____ January 4. ○ We're ○ You're ○ It's
2. Amal and Matsu are students. _____ friends. ○ They're ○ I'm ○ It's
3. Mr. Jackson is a teacher. _____ married. ○ She's ○ They're ○ He's
4. Erika and Ron are teachers. _____ divorced. ○ You're ○ They're ○ We're
5. This is my house. _____ in Mexico. ○ I'm ○ It's ○ You're
6. You and I are students. _____ friends. ○ They're ○ We're ○ It's
7. Mrs. Samuel is a teacher. _____ from Florida. ○ She's ○ They're ○ He's
8. My name is Elsa. _____ from Russia. ○ I'm ○ He's ○ She's

C Complete the sentences. Use subject pronouns and contractions of the *be* verb.

Chinh: Hi, __you're__ Amal, right?
Amal: Yes. This is Matsu. _____ a friend.
Chinh: Hello, _____ Chinh.
Matsu: Hi, _____ Matsu.
Chinh: Nice to meet you, Matsu.
Matsu: _____ nice to meet you, too.
Chinh: _____ a student at Locke Adult School.
Amal and Matsu: _____ students there, too.

Chinh: This is Yin. _____ from Vietnam.
Elsa: _____ from Vietnam, too, right?
Chinh: Yes, _____ from Vietnam, too.
Elsa: Hi, Yin. _____ Elsa. _____ a student.
Yin: Hi, Elsa. _____ a teacher.
Elsa: Nice to meet you.
Yin: _____ nice to meet you, too.

UNIT 1 Personal Information

CHALLENGE 4 ▶ Possessive adjectives

Possessive adjectives: *my, your, his, her, our, their*	
Pronoun	**Possessive adjective**
I am Amal Jahshan.	**My** first name is Amal.
You are a student.	**Your** address is 23 Fin Road.
He is a teacher.	**His** name is Mr. Jackson.
She is a student.	**Her** last name is Kusmin.
We are married.	**Our** address is 34 Walker Avenue.
They are married.	**Their** last name is Ramirez.

 Complete the sentences with possessive adjectives.

| my | your | his | her | our | their |

1. I am Ron. __My__ last name is Carter.   2. **We** are Josef and Anna. _____ last name is Linden.

3. **She** is Rosa. _____ last name is Gomez.   4. **You** are a student. _____ first name is _____.

5. **They** are Josef and Anna. _____ last name is Linden.   6. **He** is Stan. _____ last name is Parker.

B Match the sentences. Draw a line.

1. They are married.
2. We are students.
3. She is a teacher.
4. He is my friend.
5. I am from Russia.
6. You are a student.

a. My name is Elsa.
b. Your name is Matsu.
c. His name is Orlando.
d. Their last name is Linden.
e. Our school is Locke Adult School.
f. Her name is Mrs. Samuel.

C Bubble in the correct answer.

EXAMPLE: _____ first name is Amal. ● His   ○ My   ○ Their

Amal Jahshan
8237 Augustin Street
Irvine, CA 92714
Tel. 555-6733

1. _____ last name is Jahshan. ○ His   ○ My   ○ Their
2. _____ phone number is 555-6733. ○ Their   ○ Her   ○ His

Elsa Kusmin
23 San Andrew Street
Irvine, CA 92618
Tel. 555-5901

3. _____ address is 23 San Andrew Street. ○ Her   ○ Our   ○ Your
4. _____ zip code is 92618. ○ Her   ○ Their   ○ His
5. _____ phone number is 555-5901. ○ His   ○ Her   ○ Our

Jeff and Chinh
23905 Fin Road
Irvine, CA 92603
Tel. 555-3450

6. _____ address is 23905 Fin Road. ○ Their   ○ Your   ○ Her
7. _____ names are Jeff and Chinh. ○ Our   ○ Their   ○ My
8. _____ zip code is 92603. ○ Their   ○ Our   ○ My

D Complete the sentences. Use possessive adjectives.

EXAMPLE: Elsa is a student. __*Her*__ last name is Kusmin.

1. Amal is a student. _____ last name is Jahshan.
2. Elsa is my friend. _____ address is 23 San Andrew Street.
3. Jeff and Chinh are in California. _____ zip code is 92603.
4. I am a student. _____ first name is Matsu.
5. Elsa and I are students. _____ teacher is Mr. Jackson.
6. She is my friend. _____ address is 23905 Fin Road.
7. They are married. _____ last name is Ramirez.
8. You are a teacher. _____ name is Mr. Jackson.

UNIT 1 Personal Information: Review

Bubble in the correct answer.

EXAMPLE: Amal is a student. _____ is from Egypt.   ● He   ○ We   ○ They

Part 1: Subject pronouns
1. Orlando is a student. _____ is married.   ○ I   ○ They   ○ He
2. Elsa and Amal are students. _____ are single.   ○ I   ○ They   ○ We
3. Mr. Jackson is a teacher. _____ is from Florida.   ○ We   ○ He   ○ I
4. You and I are friends. _____ are in the same class.   ○ She   ○ They   ○ We
5. Elsa is single. _____ is from Russia.   ○ He   ○ She   ○ They
6. My name is Matsu. _____ am from Japan.   ○ He   ○ I   ○ We

Part 2: The verb *be*
1. I _____ a student.   ○ am   ○ is   ○ are
2. He _____ a teacher.   ○ am   ○ is   ○ are
3. We _____ friends.   ○ am   ○ is   ○ are
4. They _____ in school.   ○ am   ○ is   ○ are
5. She _____ from Florida.   ○ am   ○ is   ○ are
6. We _____ married.   ○ am   ○ is   ○ are

Part 3: Contractions with the verb *be*
1. My name is Orlando. _____ from Mexico.   ○ I'm   ○ She's   ○ You're
2. Her name is Elsa. _____ a student.   ○ We're   ○ She's   ○ You're
3. You and I are at Locke Adult School. _____ in the same class.   ○ It's   ○ We're   ○ They're
4. Today is February 16. _____ Tuesday.   ○ They're   ○ She's   ○ It's
5. Mr. Jackson is my friend. _____ a teacher.   ○ It's   ○ He's   ○ You're
6. Chinh and Elsa are students. _____ in the same class.   ○ We're   ○ He's   ○ They're

Part 4: Possessive adjectives
1. Elsa is a student. _____ last name is Kusmin.   ○ My   ○ Your   ○ Her
2. Orlando and Emilia are married. _____ last name is Ramirez.   ○ Her   ○ Their   ○ Our
3. We are students. _____ teacher is Mr. Jackson.   ○ My   ○ Our   ○ Your
4. Orlando and Amal are friends. _____ school is Locke Adult School.   ○ Her   ○ His   ○ Their
5. Yolanda is from Chile. _____ address is 2347 Oxford Drive.   ○ Her   ○ His   ○ Your
6. You are a student. _____ phone number is 555-7894.   ○ My   ○ Your   ○ Their

UNIT 2 Our Class

CHALLENGE 1 ▶ Where are you from?

Subject	Verb	from + country
I	am	from China.
You, We	are	from Cuba.
They / The students / Ron and Erika	are	from Austria.
He / The man / Antonio	is	from Italy.
She / The woman / Maria	is	from Mexico.
It / The car	is	from Brazil.

A Complete the sentences.

EXAMPLE: They __are__ __from__ __Spain__.

1. Josef and Anna / Germany

We _____ _____ _____.

2. Maria / Cuba

She _____ _____ _____.

3. my car / Brazil

It _____ _____ _____.

4. oranges / Chile

They _____ _____ _____.

5. Ron / Brazil

He _____ _____ _____.

6. your name / your country

I _____ _____ _____.

Where	Verb	Subject	from
Where	am	I	from?
	are	you, we	
	are	they / the students / Ron and Erika	
	is	he / the man / Antonio	
	is	she / the woman / Maria	
	is	it / the car	

Antonio / Italy   Lisa / Chile   Sun / China   Monika / Austria

B Match the questions and the answers.

1. Where is Antonio from?
2. Where is Lisa from?
3. Where is Sun from?
4. Where is Monika from?

a. She is from Chile.
b. He is from China.
c. She is from Austria.
d. He is from Italy.

C Complete the conversations.

Conversation 1:
Antonio: Where __are__ __you__ __from__?
Lisa: __I__ __am__ __from__ Chile.

Conversation 2:
Sun: Where _____ _____ _____?
Antonio: _____ _____ _____ Italy.

Conversation 3:
Sun: Where _____ _____ _____?
Monika: _____ _____ _____ Austria.

Conversation 4:
Monika: Where _____ _____ _____?
Sun: _____ _____ _____ China.

UNIT 2 — Our Class

Tell time

CHALLENGE 2 ▶ Tell time

Questions		
Question word(s)	*be* verb	Subject
What time	is	it (now)?
What time / When	is	your class?

Answers		
Subject	*be* verb	Time
The time	is	3:00. / three o'clock. / three P.M.
My class / It (It's)	is	at 7:30. / at seven thirty. / at seven thirty P.M.

A.M. = morning   P.M. = afternoon and night

A — What time is it now? Bubble in the correct answer.

EXAMPLE: What time is it in New York? It's _____ . ○ 10 A.M. ○ 1 A.M. ● 12 P.M.

Hawaii   California   Arizona   Texas   Florida

1. What time is it in California? It's _____ . ○ 10 A.M. ○ 1 P.M. ○ 12 P.M.
2. What time is it in Florida? It's _____ . ○ 4 A.M. ○ 3 P.M. ○ 8 A.M.
3. What time is it in Hawaii? It's _____ . ○ 10 P.M. ○ 11 P.M. ○ 12 A.M.
4. What time is it in Texas? It's _____ . ○ 9 A.M. ○ 2 P.M. ○ 3 A.M.
5. What time is it in Arizona? It's _____ . ○ 2 A.M. ○ 11 P.M. ○ 4 A.M.

B — Look at Milah's schedule. Match the correct times.

Milah's Schedule

 English class   Lunch   Work

 Morning break   Computer class   Bedtime

 Writing class   Afternoon break

1. When is her writing class?   a. At two thirty.
2. When is her bedtime?   b. At twelve.
3. When is her computer class?   c. At three.
4. When is her morning break?   d. At ten thirty.
5. When is her work?   e. At one.
6. When is her afternoon break?   f. At eight thirty.
7. When is her English class?   g. At nine.
8. When is her lunch?   h. At seven.

C What time is it now? Write the correct time using numbers and A.M. or P.M.

EXAMPLE: 9:00 A.M.

1. _____
2. _____
3. _____
4. _____
5. _____
6. _____

D Choose the correct answer. Bubble in the correct answer.

EXAMPLE: When is your lunch?   ● It's at one.   ○ It's one.

1. When is your English class?   ○ It's at nine.   ○ It's nine.
2. What time is your lunch break? ○ It's at twelve.   ○ It's twelve.
3. What time is it in New York?   ○ It's at 6 P.M.   ○ It's 6 P.M.
4. What time is your test?   ○ It's at three thirty. ○ It's three thirty.
5. What time is it in Washington? ○ It's at seven thirty. ○ It's seven thirty.
6. What time is it right now?   ○ It's at eleven.   ○ It's eleven.

UNIT 2 Our Class

CHALLENGE 3 ▶ Prepositions

in   on   between   in front of   in back of   next to

Question word	*be* verb	Subject	Subject + *be* verbs	Preposition	Noun
Where	is	the plant?	It's	on	the desk.
	are	the books?	They're	in	the bookcase.
				next to	
				in front of	
				in back of	
				between	the desk and the door.

A Complete the sentences with the prepositions on the right.

1. The file cabinets are __*in back of*__ the computers.
2. The plant is _____ the desk.
3. The teacher is _____ the door.
4. The trash can is _____ the desk and the bookcase.
5. The students are _____ the board.
6. The books are _____ the bookcase.

a. in
b. in front of
c. in back of
d. on
e. between
f. next to

B Complete the questions about the pictures in Exercise A.

EXAMPLE: Where is the __*bookcase*__? It is next to the trash can.

| file cabinets | plant | books | teacher | students | trash can |

1. Where are the _____? They are in back of the computers.
2. Where is the _____? It is on the desk.
3. Where are the _____? They are in the bookcase.
4. Where is the _____? It is between the desk and the bookcase.
5. Where are the _____? They are in front of the board.
6. Where is the _____? He is next to the door.

C Look at the picture and bubble in the correct answer.

EXAMPLE: It is on the desk.

    ○ the chair   ● the plant   ○ the clock   ○ the file cabinet

1. They're in front of the file cabinets.
   ○ the computers   ○ the chairs   ○ the books   ○ the pencils

2. It's next to the pencil sharpener.
   ○ the chair   ○ the plant   ○ the computer   ○ the pencil

3. It's on the wall.
   ○ the trash can   ○ the plant   ○ the clock   ○ the desk

4. He's between the door and the board.
   ○ the teacher   ○ the student   ○ the teachers   ○ the students

5. They're in front of the board.
   ○ the chairs   ○ the tables   ○ the students   ○ the books

6. They're in the bookcase.
   ○ the pencil   ○ the books   ○ the clock   ○ the door

7. They're in back of the computers.
   ○ the books   ○ the file cabinets   ○ the tables   ○ the chairs

8. It's on the table.
   ○ the pencil sharpener   ○ the chair   ○ the clock   ○ the trash can

Prepositions

UNIT 2 Our Class

CHALLENGE 4 ▶ Possessive forms

Possessive adjective	's (apostrophe s)
His home is in California. (Orlando)	Orlando's home is in California.
Her address is 23 San Andrew Street. (Elsa)	Elsa's address is 23 San Andrew Street.
His (or Her) class is at 8:00 A.M. (The student)	The student's class is at 8:00 A.M.
Her friends are at Florida Adult School. (My sister)	My sister's friends are at Florida Adult School.
His classes are at Florida Adult School. (Mr. Jackson)	Mr. Jackson's classes are at Florida Adult School.

A Answer the questions about Elsa and Orlando.

EXAMPLE: Where is ____**Orlando's**____ home?   His home is in California.

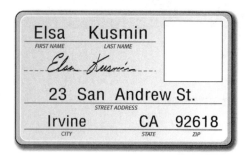 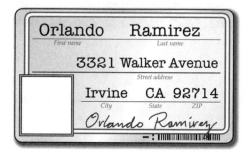

1. What is _____ address?   Her address is 23 San Andrew Street.
2. What is _____ zip code?   Her zip code is 92618.
3. What is _____ address?   His address is 3321 Walker Avenue.
4. What is _____ zip code?   His zip code is 92714.
5. What is _____ last name?   Her last name is Kusmin.
6. What is _____ last name?   His last name is Ramirez.

B Complete the sentences with the possessive form.

EXAMPLE: ____**Julie's**____ address is 564 South Street. (Julie).

1. _____ home is in California. (Orlando)
2. _____ homework is on the wall. (The student)
3. _____ friends are in Florida. (Edgar)
4. _____ classes are at 9 A.M. (Mrs. Brown)
5. _____ books are in the classroom. (The boy)
6. _____ last name is Gomez. (Concepcion)
7. _____ sister is at Locke Adult school. (My friend)
8. _____ pencils are in the bag. (Julie)

C Read the answer. Write the question.

EXAMPLE: What is ____**Concepcion's address**____? Her address is 496 Park Road.

> Concepcion Gomez, Student
> Address: 496 Park Road
> Phone: 712-555-6011

> Edgar Sebault, Student
> Address: 34 Green Avenue
> Phone: 712-555-0205

> Mr. David Jackson, Teacher
> Address: 435 Broadway Street
> Phone: 712-555-2735

1. What is _____? Her last name is Gomez.
2. What is _____? His last name is Sebault.
3. What is _____? His first name is David.
4. What is _____? His address is 435 Broadway.
5. What is _____? His address is 34 Green Avenue.
6. What is _____? His phone number is 712-555-0205.
7. What is _____? Her phone number is 712-555-6011.
8. What is _____? His phone number is 712-555-2735.

D Write the sentences with the possessive form.

EXAMPLE: Orlando is a student. His class is at 8:30 A.M.

Orlando's class is at 8:30 A.M.

1. Julie is from Canada. Her home is in Montreal.

2. Shiro is from Japan. His last name is Tanaka.

3. The teacher is in the classroom. His name is Mr. Jackson.

4. Mr. Jackson is from Florida. His address is 4345 Broadway Street.

5. The woman is driving a car. Her name is Maria.

6. My friend is a student. Her teacher is Mrs. Brown.

UNIT 2 Our Class: Review

Bubble in the correct answer.

EXAMPLE: Where _____ from?   ● is she   ○ she is

Part 1: *Where . . . from?* questions and answers

1. Where _____ from?   ○ you are   ○ are you
2. Where _____ from?   ○ is she   ○ she is
3. Where _____ from?   ○ we are   ○ are we
4. She _____ China.   ○ are from ○ is from
5. They _____ Chile.   ○ are from ○ is from
6. We _____ Canada.   ○ is from   ○ are from

Part 2: Time

1. It's _____.   ○ 3:00   ○ 5:00   ○ 8:00
2. It's _____.   ○ 1:30   ○ 2:30   ○ 5:30
3. It's _____.   ○ 1:00   ○ 11:00 ○ 9:00
4. It's _____.   ○ 10:30 ○ 11:30 ○ 12:30

Part 3: Prepositions

1. ○ in back of   ○ on   ○ between   ○ in
2. ○ next to   ○ in front of ○ between   ○ on
3. ○ next to   ○ on   ○ between   ○ in front of
4. ○ next to   ○ in   ○ between   ○ in back of

Part 4: Possessive forms

1. What is _____ address? Her address is 2347 Oxford Drive.
   ○ she   ○ Yolanda   ○ Yolanda's
2. When is _____ class? His class is at 9:00 A.M.
   ○ he   ○ Shiro   ○ Shiro's
3. My friend is a student. Her teacher is Mrs. Brown. _____ is Mrs. Brown.
   ○ My friend's teacher   ○ My teacher's friend
4. My sister is at Locke Adult School. Her friend is a student at Florida Adult School. _____ is a student at Florida Adult School.
   ○ My friend's sister   ○ My sister's friend

UNIT 3 Food

CHALLENGE 1 ▶ Negative form of the verb *be*

Subject pronoun	*be* verb + *not*		Example sentence
I	am not	hungry from Japan a teacher	I'm not hungry. I'm thirsty.
He	is not (isn't)		He's not from Japan. He's from China.
She			She's not a teacher. She's a student.
It		at 3:00 P.M.	It's not at 3:00 P.M. It's at 3:30 P.M.
We	are not (aren't)	thirsty	We're not thirsty. We're hungry.
You		from Italy	You're not from Italy. You're from France.
They		students	They're not students. They're teachers.

A Write the correct word on the line.

an apple	3:00 P.M.	divorced	hungry	a potato	thirsty
a tomato	rainy	a chicken	married	cold	4:00 P.M.
a turkey	sunny	hot	thirsty	hungry	an orange

1. He's **hungry**.
   He's not **thristy**.

2. He's **thirsty**.
   He's not _____.

3. They're _____.
   They're not _____.

4. It's _____.
   It's not _____.

5. It's _____.
   It's not _____.

6. It's _____.
   It's not _____.

7. It's _____.
   It's not _____.

8. It's _____.
   It's not _____.

9. It's _____.
   It's not _____.

Negative form of the verb be

B Write sentences with the opposite meaning.

EXAMPLE: She's not a teacher. (student) *She's a student*.

1. You're not a teacher. (student)

2. He's not from Mexico. (Ecuador)

3. It's not hot. (cold)

4. It's not 4:00 P.M. (3:00 P.M.)

5. They're not from Canada. (Australia)

6. They're not his friends. (my friends)

7. We're not hungry. (thirsty)

8. I'm not married. (single)

C Write sentences with the opposite meaning.

EXAMPLE: She is a teacher. (student) *She's not a student*.

1. He's a student. (teacher)

2. We're from Chile. (Venezuela)

3. It's 9:00 A.M. (10:00 A.M.)

4. You're from Senegal. (Morocco)

5. They're teachers. (students)

6. I'm hungry. (thirsty)

7. They're oranges. (apples)

8. She's my friend. (your friend)

UNIT 3 Food

CHALLENGE 2 ▶ *A / an* and singular / plural nouns

a	*an* (before a, e, i, o, u)
a carrot	an egg
a sandwich	an apple

Singular form	Plural form
an egg	egg**s**
a carrot	carrot**s**
Exceptions	
a tomato	tomato**es**
a potato	potato**es**
a sandwich	sandwich**es**

A Write *a* or *an*.

EXAMPLE: __an__ orange

1. _____ egg
2. _____ carrot
3. _____ onion
4. _____ sandwich
5. _____ apple

6. _____ banana
7. _____ potato
8. _____ pear
9. _____ green pepper
10. _____ cookie

UNIT 3 21

B Write *a*, *an*, or a number and the singular or plural noun.

EXAMPLE: __an__ __apple__   __6__ __apples__

C What's on your shopping list? Write *the plural form*.

EXAMPLE: (apple) Three ___apples___.

1. (orange) Two _____.
2. (tomato) Four _____.
3. (sandwich) Three chicken _____.
4. (egg) Six _____.
5. (cookie) Twelve _____.
6. (tomato) Five _____.
7. (package) Twelve _____ of cheese.
8. (banana) Two _____.
9. (potato) A bag of _____.
10. (pie) Two apple _____.

UNIT 3

UNIT 3 Food

CHALLENGE 3 ▶ Count and non-count nouns

Count nouns		Non-count nouns	
	a banana bananas		milk **Incorrect:** a milk milks
	an egg eggs		rice
	an apple apples		bread
	a tomato tomatoes		cheese
	an onion onions		spaghetti
	a cookie cookies		ice cream

A Are these food words count or non-count? Bubble in the correct answer.

EXAMPLE: banana

   ● count   ○ non-count

1. milk
   ○ count   ○ non-count
2. rice
   ○ count   ○ non-count
3. egg
   ○ count   ○ non-count
4. potato chip
   ○ count   ○ non-count
5. spaghetti
   ○ count   ○ non-count
6. chicken sandwich
   ○ count   ○ non-count
7. french fry
   ○ count   ○ non-count
8. cheese
   ○ count   ○ non-count
9. ice cream sundae
   ○ count   ○ non-count
10. butter
    ○ count   ○ non-count

Count and non-count nouns

B Write *a* or *an* in front of singular count nouns. Write ∅ in front of plural count nouns and all non-count nouns.

EXAMPLE: Andre likes __∅__ cheese.

1. Silvina wants _____ apple.
2. Maria wants _____ cookies.
3. Saul wants _____ burgers and fries.
4. Chen wants _____ milk.
5. Amadeo wants _____ chicken sandwich.
6. Yoshi wants _____ rice.
7. Andre wants _____ orange.
8. I want _____ hamburger.

	Singular verb	Plural Verb
Non-count nouns	The milk **is** in the fridge.	– (No plural)
	The cheese **is** in the sandwich.	
Count nouns	The apple **is** on the table.	The apples **are** on the table.
	The orange **is** next to the apple.	The oranges **are** next to the apples.

C Choose the correct form of the verb *be*. Bubble in the correct answer.

EXAMPLE: The bananas _____ in the basket.   ○ is   ● are

1. The butter _____ next to the chicken.   ○ is   ○ are
2. The water _____ next to the milk.   ○ is   ○ are
3. The apples _____ in the basket.   ○ is   ○ are
4. The bread _____ next to the turkey.   ○ is   ○ are
5. The potatoes _____ in the front.   ○ is   ○ are
6. The lettuce _____ in the back.   ○ is   ○ are
7. The mayonnaise _____ in the fridge.   ○ is   ○ are
8. The cheese _____ next to the tomatoes.   ○ is   ○ are
9. The turkey _____ next to the cheese.   ○ is   ○ are
10. The apples _____ next to the oranges.   ○ is   ○ are

UNIT 3 Food

CHALLENGE 4 ▶ Simple present of *like* and *want*

Simple Present		
Subject pronoun	Verb	Example sentence
I, you, we, they	like want	I like chocolate. We want fruit salad.
he, she, it	likes wants	She likes ice cream. He wants potato chips.

A Write *like* or *likes*.

1. Amadeo _____ cookies.
2. Chen _____ apple pie.
3. Saul _____ chocolate sundaes.
4. Amadeo, Chen, and Saul _____ desserts.

B Bubble in the correct answer.

EXAMPLE: Maria _____ desserts.   ○ like   ● likes

1. She _____ ice cream.   ○ like   ○ likes
2. Saul _____ cookies.   ○ like   ○ likes
3. I _____ candy.   ○ like   ○ likes
4. They _____ apple pie.   ○ like   ○ likes
5. You _____ fruit.   ○ like   ○ likes
6. Andre and Silvina _____ sundaes.   ○ like   ○ likes
7. He _____ cake.   ○ like   ○ likes
8. We _____ chocolate.   ○ like   ○ likes
9. My partner _____ chocolate ice cream.   ○ like   ○ likes
10. My partner and I _____ chocolate cake.   ○ like   ○ likes

Simple present of *like* and *want*

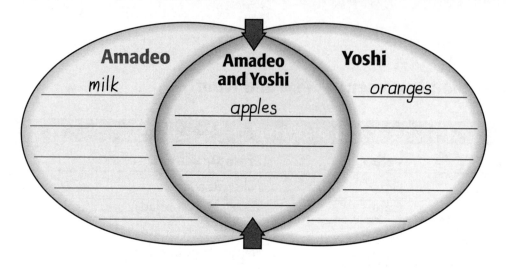

C **Look at the chart and write sentences using *like* or *likes*.**

1. Amadeo _____

2. Yoshi _____

3. Amadeo and Yoshi _____

D **Look at the two shopping lists and write sentences using *want* or *wants*.**

Silvina's Shopping List:	Andre's Shopping List:
bread	bread
milk	chicken
water	tomatoes
lettuce	water
chicken	apples

1. Andre _____

2. Silvina _____

3. Andre and Silvina _____

UNIT 3

UNIT 3 Food: Review

Bubble in the correct answer.

EXAMPLE: Amal is single. _____ married.   ○ He's   ● He's not

Part 1: Negative form of the verb *be*
1. Maria is married. _____ single.   ○ She's   ○ She's not
2. Cuba is not rainy. _____ sunny.   ○ It's   ○ It's not
3. Saul is not hungry. _____ thirsty.   ○ He's   ○ He's not
4. We're from Mexico. _____ from Chile.   ○ We're   ○ We're not
5. I am a teacher. _____ a student.   ○ I'm   ○ I'm not
6. The books are on the table. _____ in the bag. ○ They're ○ They're not

Part 2: *A / an* and singular / plural nouns
1. I want _____ apple.   ○ a   ○ an
2. I want _____ sandwich.   ○ a   ○ an
3. I want _____ egg.   ○ a   ○ an
4. I want two _____.   ○ potatos   ○ potatoes
5. I want three _____.   ○ sandwiches ○ sandwichs
6. I want six _____.   ○ tomatos   ○ tomatoes

Part 3: Count and non-count nouns
1. The apple _____ on the table.   ○ is   ○ are
2. The milk _____ next to the water.   ○ is   ○ are
3. The orange _____ in the basket.   ○ is   ○ are
4. The bananas _____ next to the apples.   ○ is   ○ are
5. The potatoes _____ next to the turkey.   ○ is   ○ are
6. The rice _____ next to the vegetables.   ○ is   ○ are

Part 4: Present simple of *like* and *want*
1. Andre _____ turkey sandwiches.   ○ like   ○ likes
2. Saul and Chen _____ desserts.   ○ like   ○ likes
3. I _____ chocolate.   ○ like   ○ likes
4. They _____ apples.   ○ want   ○ wants
5. Maria _____ fruit.   ○ want   ○ wants
6. We _____ cheese sandwiches.   ○ want   ○ wants

UNIT 4 Clothing

CHALLENGE 1 ▶ There is / There are

	There	be verb	Noun
Singular	There	is	a green shirt. one pair of socks.
Plural	There	are	two small shirts. three pairs of shoes.

Singular	A pair of... (= 2)	Singular	A pair of... (= 1)
sock	socks	–	pants
shoe	shoes	–	shorts

A Complete the sentences about the pictures.

EXAMPLE: There __is__ __one__ pair of pants.

1. There _____ _____ pairs of pants.

2. There _____ _____ shirts.

3. There _____ _____ dress.

4. There _____ _____ pair of shoes.

5. There _____ _____ pairs of socks.

6. There _____ _____ sweater.

Questions		
How many	Noun	be verb
How many	shirts medium shirts pairs of shoes	are there?

B **Complete the questions.**

1. How many __small__ __shirts__ are there? Three.
2. How many _____ _____ are there? Two.
3. How many _____ _____ are there? Two.
4. How many _____ _____ are there? One.

C **Make an inventory of clothes on pages 28 and 29. Make questions and answers about your inventory.**

EXAMPLE: How many dresses are there? There is one dress.

Inventory List	
Quantity (How many?)	Item

UNIT 4

UNIT 4 Clothing

CHALLENGE 2 ▶ Counting money

How much is it? / How much are they?	
$0.75	seventy-five cents
$22.50	twenty-two dollars and fifty cents / twenty-two fifty
$127	one hundred twenty-seven dollars

A Match the pictures with the words.

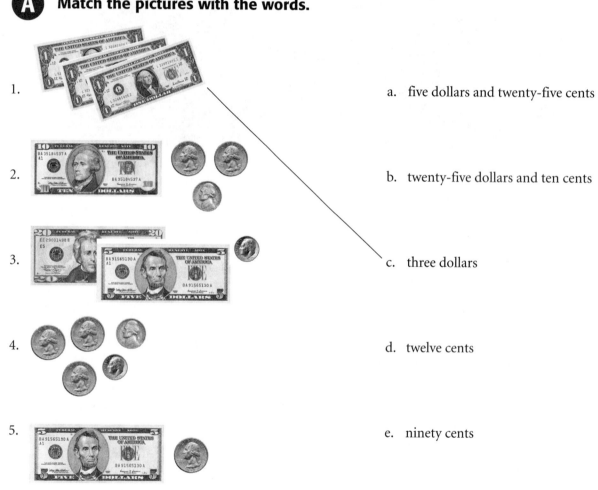

a. five dollars and twenty-five cents

b. twenty-five dollars and ten cents

c. three dollars

d. twelve cents

e. ninety cents

f. ten dollars and fifty-five cents

B Bubble in the correct answer.

EXAMPLE: $12.80
- ● twelve eighty
- ○ twelve and eighty
- ○ twelve and eighty dollars

1. $21.00
   - ○ twenty and one dollars
   - ○ twenty-one dollars
   - ○ one and twenty dollars

2. $13.25
   - ○ thirteen and twenty-five
   - ○ thirteen and twenty-five cents
   - ○ thirteen twenty-five

3. $56.90
   - ○ fifty-six and ninety
   - ○ fifty-six ninety cents
   - ○ fifty-six dollars and ninety cents

4. $0.50
   - ○ fifty cents
   - ○ five dollars
   - ○ five cents

5. $11.95
   - ○ eleven and ninety-five
   - ○ eleven ninety-five
   - ○ eleven ninety and five

6. $134
   - ○ one hundred thirty-four dollars
   - ○ one hundred and thirty-four
   - ○ a hundred thirty-four cents

C Circle the correct answer—Y (yes) or N (no).

EXAMPLE: A nickel and a dime are fifteen cents. (Y) N

1. A nickel is five cents. Y N
2. Two dimes are twenty-five cents. Y N
3. Four quarters are a dollar. Y N
4. Two dimes and a nickel are thirty-five cents. Y N
5. Three dimes and four pennies are thirty-four cents. Y N
6. Three nickels and a dime are twenty-five cents. Y N
7. Two quarters and a nickel are sixty-five cents. Y N
8. Five nickels, one dime, and two pennies are forty-seven cents. Y N

UNIT 4 Clothing

CHALLENGE 3 ▶ Questions with *How much . . . ?*

Questions		
How much	*be* verb	Noun
How much	is	the dress?
	are	the dresses?

Answers			
Singular	The dress	is	$22.50.
Plural	The dresses	are	$22.50 each.

A Look at the clothing ad. Match the questions and the answers.

1. How much are the dresses?
2. How much are the pants?
3. How much is the blouse?
4. How much are the shoes?
5. How much is the dress?
6. How much are the sweaters?
7. How much are the blouses?
8. How much is the shirt?
9. How much is the sweater?
10. How much are the shirts?

a. They're $28.
b. It's $33.
c. They're $22.50 each.
d. They're $33 each.
e. They're $24.
f. They're $40 each.
g. It's $40.
h. It's $18.
i. It's $22.50.
j. They're $18 each.

B Make questions about each picture.

EXAMPLE: How much ___*is the shirt*___ ?

1. How much _____ ?   2. How much _____ ?

3. How much _____ ?   4. How much _____ ?

5. How much _____ ?   6. How much _____ ?

C Complete the conversations.

EXAMPLE:

Sam: How much are the shirts?

Salesperson: ___*They're*___ $12 each.

1. *Maria:* How much are the sweaters?
   Salesperson: _____ $45 each.
2. *Brenda:* How much is the blouse?
   Salesperson: _____ $45.
3. *Ivan:* How much are the shoes?
   Salesperson: _____ $45 a pair.
4. *Yusuf:* How much is the coat?
   Salesperson: _____ $185.

UNIT 4 Clothing

CHALLENGE 4 ▶ What size / color? and How many . . . ?

Questions			
What	color	shirt	do you want?
	size		
How many		shirts	do you want?

Answer				
Color	I	want	a green shirt,	please.
Size	I	want	a medium shirt,	please.
Quantity	I	want	three shirts,	please.

A Complete the conversations about the clothes on the left.

EXAMPLE:

Salesperson: What color dress do you want?

Maria: I want a _____**red dress**_____, please.

Salesperson: How many dresses do you want?

Maria: I want _____**two dresses**_____, please.

L / blue

1. *Salesperson:* What size sweater do you want?
   Ivan: I want a _____, please.
   Salesperson: What color do you want?
   Ivan: I want a _____, please.

8 / red

2. *Salesperson:* What color shoes do you want?
   Yusuf: I want _____, please.
   Salesperson: What size do you want?
   Yusuf: I want size _____, please.

M

3. *Salesperson:* How many pairs of shorts do you want?
   Sam: I want _____, please.
   Salesperson: What size do you want?
   Sam: I want _____, please.

S

4. *Salesperson:* What size socks do you want?
   Brenda: I want _____, please.
   Salesperson: How many pairs do you want?
   Brenda: I want _____ , please.

B Bubble in the correct question.

EXAMPLE: I want a blue coat.
- ● What color coat do you want?
- ○ How many coats do you want?
- ○ What size coat do you want?
- ○ How much are the coats?

1. I want a green sweater.
   - ○ What color sweater do you want?
   - ○ How many sweaters do you want?
   - ○ What size sweater do you want?
   - ○ How much are the sweaters?

2. I want a pair of size 10 shoes.
   - ○ What color shoes do you want?
   - ○ How many shoes do you want?
   - ○ What size shoes do you want?
   - ○ How much are the shoes?

3. I want three shirts.
   - ○ What color shirt do you want?
   - ○ How many shirts do you want?
   - ○ What size shirt do you want?
   - ○ How much are the shirts?

C Complete the sentences.

EXAMPLE: I want a shirt. ___**What color shirt**___ do you want? Green, please.

1. I want a dress. _____ do you want? Red, please.
2. I want a coat. _____ do you want? Medium, please.
3. I want a pair of shoes. _____ do you want? Size 9, please.
4. I want some shirts. _____ do you want? Three, please.
5. I want a sweater. _____ do you want? Blue, please.
6. I want some pants. _____ do you want? Black, please.
7. I want some socks. _____ do you want? Four, please.
8. I want a blouse. _____ do you want? Large, please.

What size / color? and How many . . . ?

UNIT 4 Clothing: Review

Bubble in the correct answer.

EXAMPLE: There _____ one shirt.   ● is   ○ are

Part 1: *There is / There are*

1. There _____ three shirts.   ○ is   ○ are
2. There _____ two pairs of shoes.   ○ is   ○ are
3. There _____ five dresses.   ○ is   ○ are
4. There _____ one pair of pants.   ○ is   ○ are
5. How many coats _____ there?   ○ is   ○ are
6. How many pairs of socks _____ here?   ○ is   ○ are

Part 2: Counting money

1. $27.00
   ○ twenty and seven dollars   ○ twenty-seven dollars   ○ seven and twenty dollars
2. $19.65
   ○ nineteen and sixty-five   ○ nineteen sixty-five   ○ nineteen sixty and five
3. $0.12
   ○ twelve cents   ○ twelve dollars   ○ twenty cents
4. $5.75
   ○ five and three-quarter dollars   ○ five and seventy-five cents   ○ five seventy-five

Part 3: *How much . . . ?*

1. How much _____ the sweaters?   ○ is   ○ are
2. How much _____ the coat?   ○ is   ○ are
3. How much _____ the pair of pants?   ○ is   ○ are
4. How much _____ the shirt?   ○ is   ○ are
5. The shoes are on sale. _____ $25 each.   ○ It's   ○ They're
6. The shirt is on sale. _____ $49.   ○ It's   ○ They're

Part 4: *What size / color?* and *How many . . . ?*

1. _____ do you want? Red, please.   ○ What size   ○ What color   ○ How many
2. _____ do you want? Large, please.   ○ What size   ○ What color   ○ How many
3. _____ do you want? Four, please.   ○ What size   ○ What color   ○ How many
4. _____ do you want? Medium, please.   ○ What size   ○ What color   ○ How many

UNIT 5 Our Community

CHALLENGE 1 ▶ Questions with *Where* . . . ?

Where	*do* verb	Subject	Main verb
Where	do	I / you / we / they	live? buy food?

Subject	Main verb	Preposition	Noun
I / You / We / They	live buy food	in at	an apartment. a supermarket.

A Write the words on the line.

| rent videos | buy shoes | save money | live |

1. I _____ at a shoe store.   3. I _____ in an apartment.

2. I _____ at a video store.   4. I _____ in a bank.

B Write the words.

| buy | eat | live | mail | take |

1. Where do you ___**buy**___ clothing?   4. Where do you _____ a letter?
2. Where do we _____ food?   5. Where do they _____ lunch?
3. Where do I _____ the train?   6. Where do you _____ now?

Questions with Where....?

Where	do verb	Subject	Main verb
Where	does	Chen / he / she	live?
Where	do	I / you / we / they	eat? sleep?

Subject	Main verb	Preposition	Noun
Chen He / She	lives	in	an apartment.
Natalia and Latifa They	live	in	a house.
I / You / We	live	in	an apartment.

C Bubble in the correct answer.

EXAMPLE: Where _____ Natalia buy medicine?   ○ do   ● does

1. Where _____ Natalia live?   ○ do   ○ does
2. Where _____ Chen live?   ○ do   ○ does
3. Where _____ Chen and Natalia live?   ○ do   ○ does
4. Where _____ Natalia eat?   ○ do   ○ does
5. Where _____ Chen eat?   ○ do   ○ does
6. Where _____ Chen and Natalia buy food?   ○ do   ○ does

D Bubble in the correct answer.

EXAMPLE: Natalia _____ medicine in a pharmacy.   ○ buy   ● buys

1. Natalia _____ in an apartment.   ○ live   ○ lives
2. She _____ in a house.   ○ live   ○ lives
3. Natalia and Chen _____ in a city.   ○ live   ○ lives
4. Natalia _____ in a coffee shop.   ○ eat   ○ eats
5. Chen _____ in a fast-food restaurant.   ○ eat   ○ eats
6. They _____ food in a supermarket.   ○ buy   ○ buys

UNIT 5 Our Community

CHALLENGE 2 ▶ Questions and answers with ... or ...

		Questions			
do verb	Subject	Main verb	Preposition	Noun	*or* + Noun
Do	you	live	in	a house	or an apartment?
Do	you	take	–	the train	or the bus?

	Answers		
Subject	Main verb	Preposition	Noun
I	live	in	an apartment.
I	take	–	the train.

A Use the words from the box to make questions and answers.

EXAMPLE: *A:* Do you ____**live in an apartment or a condominium**____ ?

B: I ____**live**____ in an apartment.

| live | take | turn |

1. *A:* Do you _____ ?
   B: I _____ the bus.

2. *A:* Do you _____ ?
   B: I _____ in a house.

3. *A:* Do you _____ ?
   B: I _____ right.

Questions and answers with ... or ... ?

Questions					
do Verb	Subject	Main verb	Preposition	Noun	*or* + Noun
Does	James he, she	live	in	a house	or an apartment?
Do	I / you / we / they	live	in	a house	or an apartment?

Answers			
Subject	Main verb	Preposition	Noun
James He, She	lives	in	an apartment.
I / You / We / They	live	in	a house.

B Make questions. Answer the questions using the underlined word.

EXAMPLE: Natalia / take / <u>train</u> / bus

Q: ____***Does Natalia take the train or the bus***____ ?

A: ____***She takes the train***____ .

1. James / take / <u>bus</u> / train

   Q: _____ ?

   A: _____ .

2. Chen / work / <u>bank</u> / hospital

   Q: _____ ?

   A: _____ .

3. Latifa / live / First Street / <u>Parker Avenue</u>

   Q: _____ ?

   A: _____ .

4. Natalia and Chen / live / Casper Town / <u>Alpine City</u>

   Q: _____ ?

   A: _____ .

5. Chen / eat breakfast / coffee shop / <u>fast-food restaurant</u>

   Q: _____ ?

   A: _____ .

6. James and Chen / buy food / <u>supermarket</u> / grocery store

   Q: _____ ?

   A: _____ .

UNIT 5

UNIT 5 Our Community

CHALLENGE 3 ▶ Yes/No questions and answers with do

Questions		
do verb	**Subject**	**Main verb**
Do	I / you / we / they	drive?
		ride a bike?
Does	he / she	take the bus?
	it	cost 25 cents?

Answers		
Yes	**Subject**	**do verb**
Yes,	I / you / we / they	do.
Yes,	he / she / it	does.
No	**Subject**	**do verb + not**
No,	I / you / we / they	do not./don't.
No,	he / she / it	does not./doesn't.

A Match the questions and the answers.

1. Do you take a bus? — b. Yes, I do.
2. Does he drive a car?
3. Do they ride bikes?
4. Does it cost one dollar?
5. Do we take a train?
6. Does she take a taxi?

a. Yes, it does.
b. Yes, I do.
c. Yes, they do.
d. No, we don't.
e. No, she doesn't.
f. No, he doesn't.

B Bubble in the correct answer.

EXAMPLE: _____ you live in an apartment?   ● Do   ○ Does

1. _____ you live in a house?   ○ Do   ○ Does
2. _____ she drive to school?   ○ Do   ○ Does
3. _____ they live in Alpine City?   ○ Do   ○ Does
4. _____ it cost three dollars?   ○ Do   ○ Does
5. _____ we take a taxi?   ○ Do   ○ Does
6. _____ I turn right at the corner?   ○ Do   ○ Does
7. _____ he walk to school?   ○ Do   ○ Does
8. _____ Chen and Natalia live on First Street?   ○ Do   ○ Does

C Complete the sentences.

EXAMPLE:

___Does___ Nga take a taxi? Yes, ___he does___ .

1. _____ Natalia drive a car?
Yes, _____ .

2. _____ James take the train?
No, _____ .

3. _____ I turn left here?
Yes, _____ .

4. _____ James and Carina live in a house?
No, _____ .

5. _____ Chen and Natalia buy food at the supermarket?
Yes, _____ .

6. _____ the bus cost one dollar?
Yes, _____ .

D Write questions for these answers.

EXAMPLE: Q: ___Does he live in an apartment___ ?
A: Yes, he does. He lives in a big apartment.

1. Q: _____ ?
A: No, you don't. You turn right.

2. Q: _____ ?
A: Yes, she does. She lives in a big house.

3. Q: _____ ?
A: No, they don't. They go to school by bus.

4. Q: _____ ?
A: Yes, it does. It costs one dollar for each adult.

5. Q: _____ ?
A: Yes, we do. We take the train every day.

6. Q: _____ ?
A: No, you don't. You turn left after the supermarket.

UNIT 5 — Our Community

CHALLENGE 4 ▶ *Where* questions and *yes/no* questions with *be*

Question		
Where	**be verb**	**Subject**
Where	is	the bookstore?
	are	the taxi cabs?

Answer			
Subject	**be verb**	**Preposition**	**Place**
The bookstore	is	on	First Street.
The taxi cabs	are	next to	the supermarket.

 A Read the map. Match the questions and the answers.

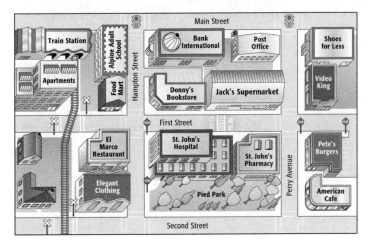

1. Where is the post office?
2. Where is the bookstore?
3. Where is the adult school?
4. Where is the video store?
5. Where is the supermarket?
6. Where is the shoe store?

a. It's next to the food mart.
b. It's on Perry and Main.
c. It's on Hampton and First.
d. It's next to the shoe store.
e. It's next to the bookstore.
f. It's on Main Street.

Questions		
be verb	**Subject**	**Place**
Is	the bank / it	on First and Main?
		next to the post office?

Where questions and yes / no questions with be

Answers	
Yes, it is.	No, it isn't.

B Answer the questions about the map on page 43.

EXAMPLE: Is the train station next to the supermarket? __**No, it isn't**__ .

1. Is the bookstore next to the bank? _____ .
2. Is the video store on Hampton and First? _____ .
3. Is the train station next to the school? _____ .
4. Is the bookstore on Perry Avenue? _____ .
5. Is the food mart on Hampton Street? _____ .
6. Is the supermarket next to the shoe store? _____ .

be verb	Subject	Place
Am	I	on First and Main?
Are	you / we	next to the post office?

Answers		
Yes	**Subject**	**Main verb**
Yes,	it	is.
Yes,	you / we	are.
Yes,	I	am.
No	**Subject**	**Main verb + *not***
No,	it	isn't.
No,	you / we	aren't.
No,	I	am not.

C Bubble in the correct form of the *be* verb.

EXAMPLE: Where _____ the post office? ○ am ● is ○ are

1. Where _____ you from? ○ am ○ is ○ are
2. What _____ your name? ○ am ○ is ○ are
3. What time _____ your lunch? ○ am ○ is ○ are
4. Where _____ the bank? ○ am ○ is ○ are
5. _____ the supermarket on the corner? ○ Am ○ Is ○ Are
6. _____ the bookstore next to the school? ○ Am ○ Is ○ Are
7. _____ the books in the bookcase? ○ Am ○ Is ○ Are
8. _____ they at the adult school? ○ Am ○ Is ○ Are

UNIT 5 — Our Community: Review

Bubble in the correct answer.

EXAMPLE: Where _____ Natalia buy clothing? ○ do   ● does

Part 1: Questions with Where . . . ?
1. Where _____ Adriano live?   ○ do   ○ does
2. Where _____ Latifa and Natalia buy food?   ○ do   ○ does
3. Where _____ you eat breakfast?   ○ do   ○ does
4. Aki _____ to school.   ○ drive   ○ drives
5. Adriano and Aki _____ in New York.   ○ live   ○ lives
6. We _____ breakfast in a coffee shop.   ○ eat   ○ eats

Part 2: Questions and answers with . . . or . . .
1. Do you _____ in an apartment or a house?   ○ live   ○ lives
2. Do I _____ left or right?   ○ turn   ○ turns
3. Does James _____ the bus or the train?   ○ take   ○ takes
4. Natalia and Chen _____ in Alpine City.   ○ live   ○ lives
5. She _____ in a restaurant.   ○ eat   ○ eats
6. Carina and Aki _____ to school.   ○ drive   ○ drives

Part 3: Yes / No questions and answers with do
1. _____ you live in a house? Yes, I do.   ○ do   ○ does
2. _____ James drive to school? No, he does not.   ○ do   ○ does
3. Do we need a taxi? Yes, we _____ .   ○ do   ○ does
4. _____ it cost two dollars? Yes, it does.   ○ do   ○ does
5. Do James and Carina live in a house? No, they _____ not.   ○ do   ○ does
6. Do I stop at the supermarket? Yes, you _____ .   ○ do   ○ does

Part 4: Where questions and yes / no questions with be
1. Where _____ the supermarket?   ○ is   ○ are
2. Where _____ the taxi cabs?   ○ is   ○ are
3. Where _____ the train station?   ○ is   ○ are
4. _____ the bookstore on the corner?   ○ Is   ○ Are
5. _____ the bank on First and Main?   ○ Is   ○ Are
6. _____ the buses near the post office?   ○ Is   ○ Are

UNIT 6 Healthy Living

CHALLENGE 1 ▶ Simple present of regular and irregular verbs

be verb

Pronoun	Verb	Example sentence
I	am	I am sick.
He / She / It	is	She is healthy.
You / We / They	are	They are not healthy.

Irregular Verbs: have / go

Pronoun	Verb	Example sentence
I / You / We / They	have / go	I have a headache.
		We go to the doctor.
He / She / It	has / goes	She has a cold.
		He goes to the hospital.

Regular Verbs: visit / see

Pronoun	Verb	Example sentence
I / You / We / They	visit / see	We visit the doctor.
He / She / It	visits / sees	He sees the doctor.

A Bubble in the correct answer.

EXAMPLE: Guillermo _____ a headache. ○ is ○ are ● has ○ have

1. Guillermo _____ sick. ○ is ○ are ○ has ○ have
2. Maritza _____ a headache. ○ is ○ are ○ has ○ have
3. John _____ a runny nose. ○ is ○ are ○ has ○ have
4. We _____ sick. ○ is ○ are ○ has ○ have
5. Huong _____ healthy. ○ is ○ are ○ has ○ have
6. Mele _____ ill. ○ is ○ are ○ has ○ have
7. They _____ a fever. ○ is ○ are ○ has ○ have
8. Julio _____ a sore throat. ○ is ○ are ○ has ○ have
9. Maria and Claudia _____ a cold. ○ is ○ are ○ has ○ have
10. We _____ very healthy. ○ is ○ are ○ has ○ have

B Read the chart and complete the sentences.

EXAMPLE: Antonio and Maritza __see__ the doctor __two times a year__.

	Guillermo	Antonio	Maritza
see the doctor / a year	1x	2x	2x
have a checkup / a year	1x	2x	1x
visit the eye doctor / a year	2x	2x	1x
go to the hospital / a year	1x	3x	1x

> 1x = once   2x = two times, twice   3x = three times

1. Guillermo _____ the doctor _____ .
2. Guillermo and Maritza _____ a checkup _____ .
3. Antonio and Guillermo _____ the eye doctor _____ .
4. Maritza _____ the eye doctor _____ .
5. Guillermo and Maritza _____ the hospital _____ .
6. Antonio _____ the hospital _____ .
7. Antonio _____ a checkup _____ .
8. Maritza _____ the doctor _____ .

C Complete the sentences with the correct form of the verbs in the box.

EXAMPLE: Shan __has__ a headache.

> be   have   go   see

1. Maritza _____ sick.
2. They _____ a backache.
3. Antonio _____ a checkup once a year.
4. She _____ the doctor once a year.
5. Julia and Maria _____ sore throats.
6. Huong _____ healthy.
7. Ayumi _____ to the hospital two times a year.
8. Hasna and Dalmar _____ ill.
9. I _____ healthy.
10. You _____ a checkup twice a year.

UNIT 6 Healthy Living

CHALLENGE 2 ▶ Present continuous

Present Continuous (right now)			
Pronoun	***be* verb**	**Base + *ing***	**Example sentence**
I	am	talking	I am talking.
He / She / It	is	sleeping	He is sleeping.
We / You / They	are	waiting	They are waiting.

A Match the person and the action.

1. Ron
2. Cindy
3. Cindy and Lisa
4. Stu, Brian, and Ray
5. Ron
6. The receptionist
7. The patients
8. The receptionist

a. is standing next to the plant.
b. are reading magazines.
c. is reading a health magazine.
d. are waiting for the doctor.
e. is writing.
f. is talking on the phone.
g. are talking.
h. is sitting at her desk.

B Write the correct form of the verb *be*.

EXAMPLE: Julio __is__ talking to the doctor.

1. Huong _____ having lunch.
2. Richard _____ sleeping.
3. Ayumi and Fred _____ waiting.
4. They _____ talking.
5. I _____ answering the phone.
6. Julio _____ reading a book.
7. Delmar and Julia _____ talking.
8. You _____ waiting.
9. He _____ writing.
10. My friend and I _____ listening.

C Complete the sentences about the picture. Use the words in the box and the correct form of the verb *be*.

EXAMPLE: Rosa __is__ __waiting__.

| read | sleep | talk | answer | wait | sit |

1. Antonio _____ _____ a magazine.
2. Rosa and Doreen _____ _____ .
3. Ben _____ _____ .
4. The receptionist _____ _____ the phone.
5. Antonio, Ben, Rosa, and Doreen _____ _____ for the doctor.
6. The receptionist _____ _____ at her desk.
7. The patients _____ _____ at the table.
8. The receptionist _____ _____ to a patient.

Present continuous

UNIT 6

UNIT 6 Healthy Living

CHALLENGE 3 ▶ Negative simple present of regular verbs

Simple Present		
Subject	**Verb**	**Example sentence**
I / You / We / They	eat	I eat three meals every day.
He / She / It	sleeps	She sleeps seven hours every night.

Negative Simple Present		
Subject	**Verb**	**Example sentence**
I / You / We / They	don't eat	We don't eat three meals every day.
He / She / It	doesn't sleep	He doesn't sleep seven hours every night.

A Bubble in the correct answer.

EXAMPLE: Julio _____ exercise every day.   ● doesn't   ○ don't

1. Ayumi and Julio _____ smoke.   ○ doesn't   ○ don't
2. He _____ have a checkup every year.   ○ doesn't   ○ don't
3. They _____ eat three meals a day.   ○ doesn't   ○ don't
4. Ayumi _____ eat fruit three times a day.   ○ doesn't   ○ don't
5. I _____ exercise every day.   ○ doesn't   ○ don't
6. We _____ sleep eight hours a day.   ○ doesn't   ○ don't
7. She _____ exercise 30 minutes a day.   ○ doesn't   ○ don't
8. Julio _____ smoke.   ○ doesn't   ○ don't

B Change the verbs to the negative form in the second sentences.

EXAMPLE: Julia exercises two times a week. She __doesn't exercise__ every day.

1. Hasna eats two meals a day. She _____ three meals a day.
2. Julia and Hasna have a checkup once a year. They _____ a checkup every month.
3. Julia and Dalmar sleep eight hours a day. They _____ ten hours.
4. Ayumi exercises three times a week. She _____ every day.
5. We see the doctor two times a year. We _____ the doctor every month.
6. I go to the sports center once a week. I _____ to the sports center every day.
7. They eat meat twice a week. They _____ meat every day.
8. My partner eats fruit for breakfast. He _____ fruit for lunch or dinner.

C **Complete the sentences about the chart. Use affirmative or negative forms.**

EXAMPLE: Lee ___*eats*___ three times a day.

	eat	exercise	sleep	smoke	see the doctor
Lee	3x a day	0 hours	5 hours	no	1x a year
Petra	3x a day	1 hour a day	7 hours	yes	1x a year
Chan	2x a day	1 hour a day	8 hours	no	2x a year

1. Petra and Lee _____ three times a day.

2. Chan _____ two times a day.

3. Lee _____ exercise.

4. Lee _____ five hours.

5. Lee and Chan _____ smoke.

6. Chan _____ the doctor two times a year.

7. Petra and Lee _____ the doctor once a year.

8. Petra _____ eight hours.

Negative simple present of regular verbs

UNIT 6

UNIT 6 Healthy Living

CHALLENGE 4 ▶ Questions with *How often...?*

Questions			
How often	***do* verb**	**Pronoun**	**Main verb**
How often	do	I / you / we / they	have a headache?
	does	he / she	

Answers		
Once a day.	Every day.	Never.
Two times a week.	Every week.	Not (very) often.
Three times a month.	Every month.	Sometimes.
Four times a year.	Every year.	

A Circle the correct form of the verb. Then answer the questions using the information in the chart.

EXAMPLE: How often do /(does)Richard eat a meal? ___*Three times a day*___ .

How often...?	Richard	Mele	Julia
eat a meal	3x a day	2x a day	2x a day
exercise	1x a week	3x a week	5x a week
have a backache	1x a year	0x a year	2x a year
go to the doctor	4x a year	4x a year	4x a year
have a checkup	1x a year	1x a year	2x a year

1. How often do / does Mele and Julia eat a meal? _____ .
2. How often do / does Richard exercise? _____ .
3. How often do / does Mele exercise? _____ .
4. How often do / does Richard have a checkup? _____ .
5. How often do / does Richard, Mele, and Julia go to the doctor? _____ .
6. How often do / does Julia have a checkup? _____ .
7. How often do / does Mele have a backache? _____ .
8. How often do / does Richard and Mele have a checkup? _____ .

B Read the charts and complete the sentences about Guillermo's and Hasna's meals.

EXAMPLE: Guillermo _____***eats vegetables***_____ three times a week.

Guillermo's Meals					
	Monday	**Tuesday**	**Wednesday**	**Thursday**	**Friday**
breakfast	toast eggs	toast eggs	toast eggs	toast eggs	toast eggs
lunch	sandwich	salad	sandwich	salad	sandwich
dinner	chicken vegetables cake	fish salad fruit	eggs vegetables cake	turkey vegetables fruit	fish salad cake

Hasna's Meals					
	Monday	**Tuesday**	**Wednesday**	**Thursday**	**Friday**
breakfast	yogurt	yogurt	yogurt	yogurt	yogurt
lunch	salad	salad	salad	salad	salad
dinner	eggs fruit	fish fruit	yogurt fruit	vegetables fruit	fish

1. Guillermo _____ _____ and _____ every morning.
2. Guillermo _____ _____ and _____ two times a week.
3. Hasna _____ _____ four times a week.
4. Hasna _____ _____ and _____ every day.
5. Hasna _____ _____ and _____ once a week.
6. Guillermo and Hasna _____ _____ two times a week.

C Write questions for each answer about Guillermo and Hasna. Use the chart in Exercise B.

EXAMPLE: _____***How often does Hasna eat yogurt***_____ ? Every morning.

1. _____ ? Every day.
2. _____ ? Sometimes.
3. _____ ? Never.
4. _____ ? Not very often.
5. _____ ? Every evening.
6. _____ ? Once a week.
7. _____ ? Not very often.
8. _____ ? Two times a week.

Questions with *How often . . . ?*

UNIT 6

UNIT 6 Healthy Living: Review

Bubble in the correct answer.

EXAMPLE: Guillermo _____ sick.   ● is   ○ are   ○ has   ○ have

Part 1: Simple present of regular and irregular verbs

1. Guillermo _____ a checkup once a year.   ○ is   ○ are   ○ has   ○ have
2. We _____ sick.   ○ is   ○ are   ○ has   ○ have
3. John and Julio _____ a cold.   ○ is   ○ are   ○ has   ○ have
4. Huong _____ to the hospital.   ○ is   ○ are   ○ goes   ○ go
5. They _____ the doctor every week.   ○ is   ○ are   ○ sees   ○ see
6. Mele _____ the hospital once a year.   ○ is   ○ are   ○ visits   ○ visit

Part 2: Present continuous

1. Huong _____ waiting.   ○ am   ○ is   ○ are
2. Richard and Ron _____ talking.   ○ am   ○ is   ○ are
3. She _____ having lunch.   ○ am   ○ is   ○ are
4. The doctor _____ talking.   ○ am   ○ is   ○ are
5. I _____ answering the phone.   ○ am   ○ is   ○ are
6. We _____ reading magazines.   ○ am   ○ is   ○ are

Part 3: Negative simple present of regular verbs

1. Hasna and Delmar _____ smoke.   ○ doesn't   ○ don't
2. Guillermo and Julio _____ eat three meals a day.   ○ doesn't   ○ don't
3. Delmar _____ smoke.   ○ doesn't   ○ don't
4. Julio _____ have a checkup every year.   ○ doesn't   ○ don't
5. Julia _____ exercise every day.   ○ doesn't   ○ don't
6. Ayumi _____ eat fruit three times a day.   ○ doesn't   ○ don't

Part 4: Questions with *How often . . . ?*

1. How often _____ Mele and Julia eat breakfast?   ○ does   ○ do
2. How often _____ Mele eat salad?   ○ does   ○ do
3. How often _____ Julio have a backache?   ○ does   ○ do
4. How often _____ she see the doctor?   ○ does   ○ do
5. How often _____ you have a checkup?   ○ does   ○ do
6. How often _____ we need medicine?   ○ does   ○ do

UNIT 7 Work

CHALLENGE 1 ▶ Wh- questions and answers with do

Wh- questions				
Question word	*do* verb	Pronoun	Main verb	Example sentence
What	do	I / you / we / they	do	What do you do?
When			start	When do we start?
Where	does	he / she / it	work	Where does she work?

Question	Answer
What do you do?	I am a doctor.
When do we start?	We start at 9 A.M.
Where does she work?	She works in a restaurant.

A Bubble in the correct answer.

EXAMPLE: I work in a bank.
- ● Where do you work?   ○ When do you start?   ○ When do you finish?

1. She is a cashier.
   ○ Where does she work?   ○ What does she do?   ○ When does she start?
2. They start at 7 A.M.
   ○ Where do they work?   ○ What do they do?   ○ When do they start?
3. I work in an office.
   ○ Where do you work?   ○ What do you do?   ○ When do you start?
4. Antonio is a nurse.
   ○ Where does he work?   ○ What does he do?   ○ When does he finish?
5. Paula and Gerry finish work at 11 P.M.
   ○ Where do they work?   ○ What do they do?   ○ When do they finish?
6. Emilio works in a supermarket.
   ○ Where does he work?   ○ What does he do?   ○ When does he start?

B Match the questions and the answers.

1. Where do you work?
2. What do you do?
3. What does he do?
4. Where do they work?
5. Where does she work?
6. When does she finish work?
7. When does he start?
8. When do we start?

a. He's a custodian.
b. They work at a school.
c. She finishes at 5 P.M.
d. I'm a manager.
e. He starts at 11 P.M.
f. We start at 9 A.M.
g. I work in a bank.
h. She works in a pharmacy.

C. Circle the correct form of the verb.

EXAMPLE: Where (do) / does they work? They work / (works) in an office.

1. Where do / does she work? She work / works in a bookstore.
2. When do / does they finish? They finish / finishes at 6 P.M.
3. What do / does Anna do? She is / are a receptionist.
4. When do / does we take a break? We take / takes a break at 10 A.M.
5. Where do / does Benny and Ron work? They work / works in a hotel.
6. What do / does you do? I am / are a student.
7. When do / does Maura start work? She start / starts at 11 A.M.
8. Where do / does you work? I work / works in a hospital.

D. Write questions and answers for the jobs in the pictures.

a. Oscar / custodian / school / 4 P.M.–9 P.M.

What ___does Oscar do___ ?   ___He is a custodian___ .
1. Where _____ ?   _____ .
2. When _____ ?   _____ .
3. When _____ ?   _____ .

b. Paula and Gerry / doctors / hospital / 6 A.M.–6 P.M.

1. What _____ ?   _____ .
2. Where _____ ?   _____ .
3. When _____ ?   _____ .
4. When _____ ?   _____ .

c. Rosa / cashier / clothing store / 8 A.M.–7 P.M.

1. What _____ ?   _____ .
2. Where _____ ?   _____ .
3. When _____ ?   _____ .
4. When _____ ?   _____ .

UNIT 7 Work

CHALLENGE 2 ▶ Yes/No questions and answers with *do*

Yes / No Questions

do Verb	Pronoun	Main verb		Example sentence
Do	I / you / we / they	work	in an office	Do you work in an office?
		start	at 9 A.M.	Do we start at 9 A.M.?
Does	he / she / it	type	letters	Does he type letters?

Question	Answer
Do you work in an office?	Yes, I do. / No, I don't.
Do we start at 9 A.M.?	Yes, we do. / No, we don't.
Does he type letters?	Yes, he does. / No, he doesn't.

A Bubble in the correct answer.

EXAMPLE: _____ he clean the floors? ○ Do ● Does

1. _____ you open the store? ○ Do ○ Does
2. _____ she type letters? ○ Do ○ Does
3. _____ they file papers? ○ Do ○ Does
4. _____ I answer the phone? ○ Do ○ Does
5. _____ Emilio count money? ○ Do ○ Does
6. _____ Carolina do her homework? ○ Do ○ Does
7. _____ we ask questions? ○ Do ○ Does
8. _____ the teacher answer the questions? ○ Do ○ Does

B Match the questions with the answers. Use the information in the chart.

	where	start	finish
Paula (She is a receptionist.)	hotel	9 A.M.	5 P.M.
Maria (She is a manager.)	restaurant	5 P.M.	1 A.M.
Alfredo (He is a custodian.)	school	9 A.M.	4 P.M.

1. Does Paula work in a hotel? — a. Yes, they do.
2. Does Maria start at 9 A.M.? — b. Yes, she does.
3. Do Paula and Alfredo start at 9 A.M.? c. Yes, she does.
4. Does Maria finish at 1 A.M.? d. No, she doesn't.
5. Does Alfredo work in a school? e. No, he doesn't.
6. Do Alfredo and Paula work in a restaurant? f. Yes, she does.
7. Does Alfredo finish at 5 P.M.? g. No, they don't.
8. Does Paula finish at 5 P.M.? h. Yes, he does.

C Answer the questions.

EXAMPLE: Does Chan answer questions? __*Yes, he does*__ .

Chen: drives a bus, answers questions, counts money

Louisa: answers questions, talks to customers, counts money

Vache: answers questions, talks to customers, answers the phone, counts money

1. Does Chan answer the phone? _____ .
2. Do Luisa and Vache talk to customers? _____ .
3. Does Luisa answer the phone? _____ .
4. Does Luisa drive a bus? _____ .
5. Does Vache answer the phone? _____ .
6. Do Chan and Luisa answer the phone? _____ .
7. Do Luisa and Vache count money? _____ .
8. Do Chan, Luisa, and Vache answer questions? _____ .

D Change the sentences into *yes/no* questions and answers.

EXAMPLE: Amy doesn't answer the phone.

_____***Does she answer the phone***_____ ? _____***No, she doesn't***_____ .

1. She files papers.
   _____ ? _____ .

2. They talk to customers.
   _____ ? _____ .

3. I take a lunch break at 1 P.M.
   _____ ? _____ .

4. They don't come to work on time.
   _____ ? _____ .

5. She doesn't clean the office.
   _____ ? _____ .

6. Mr. Brown doesn't type letters.
   _____ ? _____ .

7. We work on Sunday.
   _____ ? _____ .

8. You work here every day.
   _____ ? _____ .

UNIT 7 Work

CHALLENGE 3 ▶ Modal Verb: *can* and *can't*

can and can't				
Pronoun	**Can**	**Main verb**	**Example sentence**
I / You / He / She / It / We / They	can	count	She can count money.
		speak	We can speak English.
	can't (cannot)	count	He can't count money.
		speak	They can't speak English.

Yes/No Questions with *can*			
Can	**Pronoun**	**Main verb**	**Example question**
Can	I / you / he / she / it / we / they	count	Can she count money?
		speak	Can they speak English?

Question	Answer
Can she count money?	Yes, she can. / No, she can't.
Can they speak English?	Yes, they can. / No, they can't.

 A Complete the chart with information about yourself. Then complete the sentences with *can* or *can't*. Use the information in the chart.

EXAMPLE: Emilio __can't__ type.

	Emilio	Carolina	You
type	no	yes	
drive	yes	yes	
count money	yes	no	
use a computer	yes	yes	

1. Carolina _____ type.
2. Emilio _____ drive.
3. Emilio and Carolina _____ drive.
4. Carolina _____ count money.
5. Emilio _____ count money.
6. Carolina _____ use a computer.
7. Emilio _____ use a computer.
8. Emilio and Carolina _____ use a computer.

Complete the information about yourself.
1. I _____ type.
2. I _____ drive.
3. I _____ count money.
4. I _____ use a computer.

Modal Verb: can and can't

B Complete the sentences. Use *can* or *can't* and the verbs in the box.

EXAMPLE: Emilio is a cashier. He __can__ __count__ money.

| drive | help | come | type | speak |

1. Emilio is sick. He _____ _____ to work today.
2. Carolina is a good student. She _____ _____ English.
3. Vache is a good salesperson. Emilio is a good cashier. They _____ _____ customers.
4. Chan is a good driver. He _____ _____ a bus.
5. Hue is a good doctor. Lisa is a good nurse. They _____ _____ patients.
6. Amy is a good receptionist. She _____ _____ very quickly.
7. I am a new student. I _____ _____ English.
8. Hue's children are sick. He _____ _____ to school today.

C Change the sentences into *yes/no* questions and short answers.

EXAMPLE: Emilio can't type.

_____**Can Emilio type**_____ ? __**No, he can't**__ .

1. Amy can use a computer.
   _____ ? _____ .
2. They can't count money.
   _____ ? _____ .
3. Chan can speak English.
   _____ ? _____ .
4. Emilio and Vache can answer the phone.
   _____ ? _____ .
5. You can't drive.
   _____ ? _____ .
6. We can help customers.
   _____ ? _____ .
7. Pete and Maria can't speak Spanish.
   _____ ? _____ .
8. I can type letters.
   _____ ? _____ .

UNIT 7

UNIT 7 Work

CHALLENGE 4 ▶ Affirmative and negative commands

Affirmative Commands

Pronoun	Verb		Example sentence
~~You~~	Wash	your hands	Wash your hands.
	Answer	the phone	Answer the phone.
	Type	the letters	Type the letters.

Note: "Please, wash your hands" is more polite.

Negative Commands

Pronoun	Verb		Example sentence
~~You~~	Don't (do not) wash	your hands	Don't wash your hands.
	Don't (do not) answer	the phone	Don't answer the phone.
	Don't (do not) type	the letters	Don't type the letters.

Note: "Please, don't wash your hands" is more polite.

A Match the jobs with the commands. Write the answers in the chart below.

1. custodian	*d, i*
2. receptionist	
3. cashier	
4. doctor	
5. salesperson	
6. bus driver	

a. Answer the phones.
b. Count the money.
c. Talk to the patients.
d. Clean the floors.
e. Drive carefully.
f. Help the customers.
g. Look at street signs.
h. Give change.
i. Fix the broken chairs.
j. File the papers.
k. Write the symptoms.
l. Check the inventory.

B Where do you see these signs? Use the words in the box to complete the answers.

| restaurant | office | bus | street | school |

1. Don't smoke. _____ **restaurant, office, bus, school** _____

2. Don't eat. _____

3. Wash your hands. _____

4. Stop. _____

C Complete the sentences about the receptionist and the student. Use the affirmative or negative form of the verbs in the box.

EXAMPLE: _____**Don't smoke**_____ in the office.

Receptionist:

| eat | take | answer | talk | come |

1. _____ lunch at your desk.
2. _____ the phones.
3. _____ to customers.
4. _____ to work late.
5. _____ a two-hour lunch break.

Student:

| forget | ask | do | speak | come |

1. Please, _____ to class late.
2. Please, _____ your homework.
3. Please, _____ English in class.
4. Please, _____ your books.
5. Please, _____ questions.

Affirmative and negative commands

UNIT 7

UNIT 7 Work: Review

Bubble in the correct answer.

EXAMPLE: Where _____ Emilio work?   ○ do   ● does

Part 1: *Wh-* questions and answers with *do*
1. Where _____ Vache work?   ○ do   ○ does
2. She _____ in a bookstore.   ○ work   ○ works
3. What _____ Anna and Serena do?   ○ do   ○ does
4. When _____ we take a break?   ○ do   ○ does
5. We _____ at 6 A.M.   ○ start   ○ starts
6. I _____ to the customers.   ○ talk   ○ talks

Part 2: *Yes/No* questions and answers with *do*
1. Do you start at 9 A.M.? Yes, I _____ .
   ○ do   ○ does   ○ doesn't   ○ don't
2. Does Amy answer the phone? No, she _____ .
   ○ do   ○ does   ○ doesn't   ○ don't
3. Do Emilio and Carolina type letters? Yes, they _____ .
   ○ do   ○ does   ○ doesn't   ○ don't
4. Do we answer the phone? No, we _____ .
   ○ do   ○ does   ○ doesn't   ○ don't

Part 3: Modal verb: *can* and *can't*
1. Chan is a good driver. He _____ a drive a bus.   ○ can   ○ can't
2. Hue is a good doctor. She _____ help patients.   ○ can   ○ can't
3. Carolina is sick today. She _____ come to class.   ○ can   ○ can't
4. Sulin and Tan are new students. They _____ speak English.   ○ can   ○ can't
5. Can you help me? Yes, I _____ .   ○ can   ○ can't
6. Can Emilio write letters? No, he _____ .   ○ can   ○ can't

Part 4: Affirmative and negative commands
1. Restaurant manager: _____ your hands.   ○ Wash   ○ Don't wash
2. Receptionist: _____ a very long lunch break.   ○ Take   ○ Don't take
3. Bus driver: _____ in the bus.   ○ Smoke   ○ Don't smoke
4. Office manager: _____ to work late.   ○ Come   ○ Don't come
5. Teacher: Please _____ questions.   ○ ask   ○ don't ask
6. Teacher: Please _____ your homework.   ○ do   ○ don't do

UNIT 8 Lifelong Learning

CHALLENGE 1 ▶ Review: Containers / measurements with count and non-count nouns

Count Noun	Package or Container
a divider / some dividers	• a set of dividers • two sets of dividers

Non-count Noun	Package or Container
paper	• a sheet of paper • two sheets of paper

A Describe the pictures with the words from the box.

| box | bottle | set | jar | pair | package |

1. _____**two pairs of pants**_____   3. _____

2. _____   4. _____

5. _____   7. _____

6. _____   8. _____

Adjectives with Numbers

Article	(number)-(singular noun)	Noun	Noun phrase
a	10-dollar	bill	a 10-dollar bill
a	twenty-minute	break	a twenty-minute break

B **Rewrite these sentences. Use adjectives with numbers.**

EXAMPLE: My coffee break is ten minutes. I have a ___**ten-minute coffee break**___ .

1. My lunch break is 45 minutes. I have a _____ .
2. My apartment has three bedrooms. I have a _____ .
3. My binder is 2 inches. I have a _____ .
4. My appointment is ten minutes. I have a _____ .
5. My cassette tape is ninety minutes. I have a _____ .
6. My notebook has 200 pages. I have a _____ .

C **Match the questions and the answers.**

1. Do you live in an apartment?   a. I want one set, please.
2. How many dividers do you want?   b. Yes, it's a one-bedroom.
3. How much tomato sauce do you want?   c. OK, I have a one-hour lunch break.
4. What kind of change do you need?   d. One 200-sheet package, please.
5. Do you have time to go out to eat?   e. I want two jars, please.
6. How much paper do you want?   f. Two ten-dollar bills, please.

Review: Containers / measurements with count and non-count nouns

UNIT 8

UNIT 8 Lifelong Learning

CHALLENGE 2 ▶ Review: *Wh-* questions with *be* and *do*

Wh- Questions with Main Verbs				
Question word	***do* verb**	**Pronoun**	**Main verb**	**Example sentence**
What	do	I / you / we / they	do	What do you do?
When			start	When do we start?
Where			work	Where do they work?
How many hours	does	he / she / it	study	How many hours does she study?
How often			eat	How often does he eat?
How much			cost	How much does it cost?

Question word	***be* verb**		**Example sentence**
What	is	he / she / it / your name	What is your name?
When			
Where	are	you / we / they / the books	Where are the books?

A Match the questions and the answers.

1. Where do you live?
2. When does your class start?
3. What is your name?
4. Where are you from?
5. How much does the bus cost?
6. What do you do?
7. How many hours do you study?
8. How often do you exercise?

a. Octavio.
b. I'm a student.
c. Three hours a day.
d. In Casper Town.
e. At 8:00 A.M.
f. Three times a week.
g. $1.50.
h. Columbia.

B Write questions for the following answers.

EXAMPLE: Her name is Carina.
   What is her name ?

1. My name is Liang.
   _____ ?

2. She starts at 8:00 A.M.
   _____ ?

3. Their school is on First Street.
   _____ ?

4. Paul studies four hours a day.
   _____ ?

5. Our class is on Wednesday.
   _____ ?

6. We have breaks three times a day.
   _____ ?

7. I am a cashier.
   _____ ?

8. They work in a restaurant.
   _____ ?

C Write questions and answers about Emilio.

Name: Emilio Sanchez
Address: 435 West Pine Street
City: Alpine City
Occupation: cashier at Ultra Supermarket
Checkup: once a year
Study: three hours a day
English class: 7 A.M.–8.00 A.M.
Bus: $1.25

EXAMPLE: What __is his name__ ? __His name is__ Emilio.

1. Where _____ live? He _____ in _____ .
2. What _____ ? His address _____ .
3. How often _____ have a checkup?
   He _____ .
4. How often _____ study?
   He _____ .
5. When _____ ?
   _____ .
6. When _____ ?
   _____ .
7. How _____ school?
   _____ .
8. How much _____ ?
   _____ .

UNIT 8 Lifelong Learning

CHALLENGE 3 ▶ Review: Simple present and present continuous

Simple Present		
Pronoun	**Verb**	**Example sentence**
I / You / We / They	sleep / eat / exercise	I sleep six hours a night.
He / She / It	sleeps / eats / exercises	He exercises three hours a day.
Spelling: watch—watches, go—goes, do—does, study—studies		

Present Continuous (now, at the moment, today)			
Pronoun	***be* verb**	**Base verb + *ing***	**Example sentence**
I	am	reading	I am reading.
He / She / It	is	watching	He is watching TV.
We / You / They	are	studying	They are studying.
Spelling: exercise—exercising, write—writing, take—taking, drive—driving			

A Bubble in the correct answer.

EXAMPLE: We _____ English every day.   ● speak   ○ are speaking

1. Liang _____ three hours a day.   ○ studies   ○ is studying
2. Octavio and Liang _____ binders in the store now.   ○ buy   ○ are buying
3. Three students in our class _____ every day.   ○ exercise   ○ are exercising
4. Octavio _____ eight hours a night.   ○ sleeps   ○ is sleeping
5. Carina _____ the newspaper now.   ○ reads   ○ is reading
6. The students _____ to the teacher right now.   ○ listen   ○ are listening
7. I _____ TV now.   ○ watch   ○ am watching
8. We _____ to school five days a week.   ○ go   ○ are going

B Practice irregular spelling. Complete the sentences.

EXAMPLE: Carina (go) __*goes*__ to school every day.

a. Simple Present

1. She (go) _____ to school every day.
2. Paula (watch) _____ TV every day.
3. Octavio (study) _____ three hours every day.
4. Linda (do) _____ her homework every night.

b. Present Continuous

EXAMPLE: Carina (go) ____**is going**____ to school right now.

5. The students (exercise) _____ in the gym at the moment.
6. Liang (write) _____ a letter right now.
7. Paul and Julio (take) _____ a break today.
8. Chan (drive) _____ a bus right now.

C. Write the simple present or present continuous form of the verb.

EXAMPLE: Linda (read) ____**reads**____ a book every month.

1. Octavio (speak) _____ English every day.
2. I (write) _____ to my girlfriend at the moment.
3. The teacher (watch) _____ a video now.
4. Octavio and Liang (go) _____ to school at 8:00 A.M.
5. We (read) _____ in the morning.
6. They (study) _____ grammar today.
7. You (eat) _____ three times a day.
8. He (watch) _____ TV every night.

D. Complete the paragraph about Liang's daily schedule. Use the verbs from the box.

LIANG'S SCHEDULE

	Sunday	Monday	Tuesday	Wednesday	Thursday	Friday	Saturday
6:00 A.M.	Breakfast	Breakfast	Breakfast	Breakfast	Breakfast	Breakfast	Breakfast
9:00 A.M.		School	School	School	School	Study	Study
11:00 A.M.	Lunch	Lunch	Lunch	Lunch	Lunch	Lunch	Lunch
1:00 P.M.		Study	Study	Study	Study	Study	Study
3:00 P.M.							
5:00 P.M.		Work	Work	Work	Work	Work	
7:00 P.M.	Dinner	Dinner	Dinner	Dinner	Dinner	Dinner	Dinner
9:00 P.M.							

work	eat	study	have	go	study

Liang is a good student. He _____ breakfast at 6 A.M. every day. He _____ to school four times a week. He _____ lunch at 11 A.M. He _____ from 1 P.M. to 3 P.M. every day except Sunday. He _____ from 5 P.M. to 7 P.M. Monday to Friday. Right now it is 9:30 A.M. on Saturday, and Liang _____ .

E. Write a paragraph about your weekly schedule and describe what you are doing right now.

_____
_____
_____
_____

Review: Simple present and present continuous

UNIT 8 Lifelong Learning

CHALLENGE 4 ▶ Review: Negative forms of *be* and *do*

Negative Simple Present of Main Verbs		
Subject	***do* verb + *not* + main verb**	**Example sentence**
I / You / We / They	don't (do not) eat	We don't eat three meals every day.
He / She / It	doesn't (does not) sleep	He doesn't sleep seven hours every night.

Negative Simple Present of *be*			
Subject	***be* verb + *not***		**Example sentence**
I	am not (I'm not)	thirsty	I am not (I'm not) thirsty.
He / She / It	is not (isn't)	from China a student 3:30 P.M.	He is not (isn't) from China. She is not (isn't) a student. It is not (isn't) 3:30 P.M.
You / We / They	are not (aren't)	hungry from France teachers	We are not (aren't) hungry. You are not (aren't) from France. They are not (aren't) teachers.

A Bubble in the correct answer.

EXAMPLE: Octavio _____ study eight hours a day. ○ isn't ● doesn't

1. Pete _____ a student. ○ isn't ○ doesn't
2. Liang _____ sleep eight hours a day. ○ isn't ○ doesn't
3. Carina _____ from Russia. ○ isn't ○ doesn't
4. My friend _____ eat lunch every day. ○ isn't ○ doesn't
5. I _____ have class tomorrow. ○ am not ○ don't
6. Chan and Emilio _____ hungry. ○ aren't ○ don't
7. We _____ speak Spanish. ○ aren't ○ don't
8. You _____ go to school by bus. ○ aren't ○ don't

B Complete the sentences with the negative form of *be* or *do*.

EXAMPLE: Chan is a bus driver. He __*isn't*__ a cashier.

1. Carina and Maria are students. They _____ teachers.
2. Liang and Octavio work at night. They _____ go to school at night.
3. My teacher is from Florida. He _____ from California.
4. I am hungry. I _____ thirsty.
5. My friend eats in the evening. He _____ eat lunch.
6. He speaks English. We _____ speak Russian.

C Read the chart about Liang and Octavio. Then complete the sentences with the positive or negative form of the verb.

EXAMPLE: Liang (sleep) ___*sleeps seven hours a night*___ .

	Liang	Octavio
sleeps	seven hours	nine hours
exercises	0 times a week	5 times a week
studies at home	3 hours a day	0 hours a day
checkup	once a year	once a year
go to school	by bus / 85 cents	by bicycle / 0 cents

1. Octavio (sleep) _____.
2. Liang (sleep) _____ nine hours a night.
3. Liang (exercise) _____.
4. Octavio (exercise) _____.
5. Liang (study) _____.
6. Octavio (study) _____.
7. Liang and Octavio (have a checkup) _____.
8. Liang (go to school) _____.
9. The bus (cost) _____.
10. Octavio and Liang (walk to school) _____.

D Use the information about Hue and Vache to complete the sentences with the positive or negative form of the verb.

Hue Tran
Doctor
St. Francis Hospital
6 A.M.–7 P.M.

Vache Kronsky
Salesperson
Edy's Emporium
9 A.M.–6 P.M.

1. Hue (be) _____ a doctor.
2. Vache (be) _____ a doctor.
3. Hue's last name (be) _____ Tran.
4. Vache's last name (be) _____ Kronsky.
5. Hue (work) _____ at Edy's Emporium.
6. Vache (start) _____ at 6 A.M.
7. Hue (finish) _____ at 6 P.M.
8. Hue (finish) _____ at 7 P.M.

UNIT 8 Lifelong Learning

Bubble in the correct answer.

EXAMPLE: Do you have _____ of dividers?   ● a set   ○ a bottle   ○ a pair

Part 1: Containers / measurements with count and non-count nouns

1. I need _____ of tomato sauce.   ○ a jar   ○ a package   ○ a pair
2. Do you have _____ of aspirin?   ○ a bottle   ○ a set   ○ a package
3. How many _____ of pants do you want?   ○ pairs   ○ packages   ○ sets
4. We have a _____ coffee break.   ○ ten minutes   ○ ten-minutes   ○ ten-minute
5. You need a _____ cassette tape.   ○ sixty-minutes   ○ sixty-minute   ○ sixty minute
6. Do you have a _____ bill?   ○ twenty dollars   ○ twenty-dollars   ○ twenty-dollar

Part 2: Wh- questions with be and do

1. What's your name?   ○ a cashier   ○ every day   ○ Carina
2. Where do you live?   ○ three times a day   ○ in Alpine City   ○ by bus
3. How often do you exercise?   ○ two times a week   ○ three hours   ○ at 6 P.M.
4. How do you go to school?   ○ $1.50   ○ on Monday   ○ by car
5. Where is your school?   ○ on Perry Avenue   ○ at 8 A.M.   ○ two times a week
6. When does your class start?   ○ by bus   ○ in Alpine City   ○ at 7 A.M.

Part 3: Simple present and present continuous

1. Liang and Octavio _____ English every day.   ○ studies   ○ study   ○ is studying   ○ are studying
2. Carina _____ paper in the store right now.   ○ buys   ○ buy   ○ is buying   ○ are buying
3. Liang _____ eight hours a night.   ○ sleeps   ○ sleep   ○ is sleeping   ○ are sleeping
4. We _____ to school five days a week.   ○ goes   ○ go   ○ is going   ○ are going

Part 4: Negative forms of be and do

1. Carina _____ want to study at night.   ○ isn't   ○ doesn't
2. We _____ have class tomorrow.   ○ aren't   ○ don't
3. Mr. Jackson _____ a student.   ○ isn't   ○ doesn't
4. Chan _____ a cashier.   ○ isn't   ○ doesn't
5. The students _____ hungry.   ○ aren't   ○ don't
6. I _____ go to school by car.   ○ am not   ○ don't

APPENDIX

▶ GLOSSARY OF GRAMMAR TERMS

adjective	a word that describes a noun (Example: the *red* hat)
adverb	a word that modifies a verb, adjective, or another adverb (Example: She eats *quickly*.)
affirmative	not negative and not a question (Example: *I like him.*)
apostrophe	a punctuation mark that shows missing letters in contractions or possession (Example: *It's* or *Jim's*)
article	words used before a noun (Example: *a*, *an*, *the*)
base form	the main form of a verb, used without *to* (Example: *be*, *have*, *study*)
comma	the punctuation mark (,) used to indicate a pause or separation (Example: I live in an apartment, and you live in a house.)
complement	a word or words that add to or complete an idea after the verb (Example: He is *happy*.)
conjugation	the form of a verb (Example: I *am*, You *are*, We *are*, They *are*, He *is*, She *is*, It *is*)
conjunction	a type of word that joins other words or phrases (Example: Maria *and* Gilberto)
continuous form	a verb form that expresses action during time (Example: He *is shopping*.)
contraction	shortening of a word, syllable, or word group by omission of a sound or letter (Example: It is = *It's*, does not = *doesn't*)
count nouns	nouns that can be counted by number (Example: one *apple*, two *apples*)
definite article	use of *the* when a noun is known to speaker and listener (Example: I know *the* store.)
exclamation mark	a punctuation symbol marking surprise or emotion (Example: Hello*!*)
formal	polite or respectful language (Example: *Could* you *please* give me that?)
imperative	a command form of a verb (Example: *Listen*! or *Look out*!)
indefinite article	*a* or *an* used before a noun when something is talked about for the first time or when *the* is too specific (Example: There's *a* new restaurant.)
infinitive	the main form of a verb, usually used with *to* (Example: I like *to run* fast.)
informal	friendly or casual language (Example: *Can* I have that?)
irregular verb	a verb different from regular form verbs (Example: be = *am, are, is, was, were, being*)
modal auxiliary	a verb that indicates a mood (ability, possibility, etc.) and is followed by the base form of another verb (Example: I *can read* English well.)
modifier	a word or phrase that describes another (Example: a *good* friend)
negative	the opposite of affirmative (Example: She *does not* like meat.)
noun	a name of a person, place, thing (Example: *Joe*, *England*, *bottle*)

Glossary of grammar terms

non-count nouns	nouns impossible or difficult to count (Example: <u>*water*</u>, <u>*love*</u>, <u>*rice*</u>, <u>*fire*</u>)
object, direct	the focus of a verbs action (Example: I eat <u>*oranges*</u>.)
object pronoun	replaces the noun taking the action (Example: *Julia* is nice. I like <u>*her*</u>.)
past tense	a verb form used to express an action or state in the past (Example: You <u>*worked*</u> yesterday.)
period	a punctuation mark of a dot ending a sentence (.)
plural	indicating more than one (Example: *pencil<u>s</u>*, *child<u>ren</u>*)
possessive adjective	an adjective expressing possession (Example: <u>*our*</u> car)
preposition	a word that indicates relationship between objects (Example: <u>*on*</u> the *desk*)
present tense	a verb tense representing the current time, not past or future (Example: They <u>*are*</u> at home right now.)
pronoun	word used in place of a noun (Example: *Ted* is 65. <u>*He*</u> is retired.)
question form	to ask or look for an answer (Example: <u>*Where is my book?*</u>)
regular verb	verb with endings that are regular and follow the rule (Example: work = *work*, *work<u>s</u>*, *work<u>ed</u>*, *work<u>ing</u>*)
sentence	a thought expressed in words, with a subject and verb (Example: <u>*Julia works hard*</u>.)
short answer	a response to a *yes/no* question, usually a subject pronoun and auxiliary verb (Example: <u>*Yes, I am.*</u> or <u>*No, he doesn't.*</u>)
singular	one object (Example: <u>*a cat*</u>)
statement	a sentence or thought (Example: <u>*The weather is rainy today.*</u>)
subject	the noun that does the action in a sentence (Example: <u>*The gardener*</u> works here.)
subject pronoun	a pronoun that takes the place of a subject (Example: *John* is a student. <u>*He*</u> is smart.)
syllable	a part of a word as determined by vowel sounds and rhythm (Example: *<u>ta</u>-<u>ble</u>*)
tag questions	short informal questions that come at the end of sentences in speech (Example: You like soup, <u>*don't you?*</u> They aren't hungry, <u>*are they?*</u>)
tense	the part of a verb that shows the past, present, or future time (Example: He *talk<u>ed</u>*.)
verb	word describing an action or state (Example: The boys <u>*walk*</u> to school. I <u>*am*</u> tired.)
vowels	the letters <u>*a, e, i, o, u,*</u> and sometimes *y*
wh- questions	questions that ask for information, usually starting with *Who*, *What*, *When*, *Where*, or *Why*. (Example: <u>*Where*</u> do you live?) *How* is often included in this group.
yes/no questions	questions that ask for an affirmative or a negative answer (Example: Are you happy?)

GRAMMAR REFERENCE

The Simple Present – be

Subject	Verb	Example sentence
I	am ('m)	I am (I'm) Roberto.
you, we, they	are ('re)	You are (You're) a student. We are (We're) happy.
he, she, it	is ('s)	She is (She's) from Mexico.

The Simple Present – be (negative)

Subject	Verb	Example sentence
I	am ('m) not	I am not (I'm not) hungry.
you, we, they	are ('re) not	You are not (aren't) from Mexico.
he, she, it	is ('s) not	She is not (isn't) a student.

The Simple Present – have

Subject	Verb	Example sentence
I, you, we, they	have	I have three brothers. We have a cat.
he, she, it	has	He has free time. She has black hair.

The Simple Present – have (negative)

Subject	do + not	Verb	Example sentence
I, you, we, they	do not (don't)	have	I do not (don't) have children. We do not (don't) have a dog.
he, she, it	does not		He does not (doesn't) have blond hair.

The Simple Present – Regular verbs

Subject	Verb	Object
I, you, we, they	bring eat like	sandwiches lunch green salad
he, she, it	brings eats likes	

The Simple Present – Regular verbs (negative)

Subject	do + not	Verb	Object
I, you, we, they	do not (don't)	bring eat like	sandwiches lunch green salad
he, she, it	does not (doesn't)		

The Simple Present (yes/no question forms with do)

do	Subject	Base	Object	Example question
do	I, you, we, they	like	technology	Do you like technology?
does	he, she, it	have	a diploma	Does he have a diploma?

The Present Continuous

Subject	be	Base + ing	Example sentence
I	am	calling	I am calling about the apartment.
you, we, they	are	working	They are looking for a house.
he, she, it	is	looking	She is working right now.

Imperative form

(You)	Base	Example sentence
	chop	Chop the potatoes.

APPENDIX A-3

Grammar reference

Imperative form (negative)

(You)	do + not (don't)	Base	Example sentence
	do not (don't)	boil	Do not (don't) boil the water.

Modal Verbs (affirmative and negative forms)

Subject	Modal	Base	Example sentence
I, you, he, she, it, we, they	should should not (shouldn't)	rest go out	He should rest. You should not (shouldn't) go out.
I, you, he, she, it, we, they	can cannot (can't)	drive type	I can drive. She cannot (can't) type.
I, you, he, she, it, we, they	must must not	wear enter	You must wear eye protection. We must not enter this area.
I, you, he, she, it, we, they	will will not (won't)	study move	They will study English next year. He will not (won't) move to Florida.

The Modal Verb – should (Wh- question form)

Question word	Modal	Subject	Base	Example question
What	should	I, you, he, she, it, we, they	do?	What should I do?

Verb + infinitive

Subject	Verb	Infinitive (to + base)		Example sentence
I, you, we, they	want	to	exercise	I want to exercise.
he, she, it	wants		walk	She wants to walk.

Possessive adjectives

Subject pronoun	Possessive adjective	Example sentence
I	my	*My* shirt is blue. *My* shoes are black.
you	your	*Your* baseball cap is blue. *Your* shorts are brown.
he	his	*His* belt is black. *His* sandals are brown.
she	her	*Her* blouse is pink. *Her* shoes are white.
it	its	*Its* label is red. *Its* doors are green.
we	our	*Our* house is white. *Our* books are blue.
they	their	*Their* school is in Center City. *Their* children are happy.

Demonstrative adjectives

	Near the speaker	Away from the speaker	Example sentence
Singular	this	that	I want *this* umbrella and *that* cap.
Plural	these	those	I want *these* jeans and *those* socks.

APPENDIX